footnotes
six choreographers inscribe the page

Critical Voices in Art, Theory and Culture
A series edited by Saul Ostrow

douglas dunn
marjorie gamso
ishmael houston-jones
kenneth king
yvonne meier
sarah skaggs

essays

footnotes
six choreographers
inscribe the page

text and commentary
elena alexander

foreword
jill johnston

Australia · Canada · China · France · Germany · India · Japan · Luxembourg
Malaysia · The Netherlands · Russia · Singapore · Switzerland · Thailand

G+B
ARTS
INTERNATIONAL

Copyright © 1998 OPA
(Overseas Publishers Association) N.V.
Published by license under the G+B Arts International imprint,
part of The Gordon and Breach Publishing Group.

Frontispiece: The Tomb of Antonio Rossellino
for the Cardinal of Portugal.
Photograph: Clarence Kennedy, courtesy of
The Metropolitan Museum of Art.

Printed in Canada.

Amsteldijk 166
First Floor
1079 LH Amsterdam
The Netherlands

British Library Cataloguing in Publication Data
Footnotes : six choreographers inscribe the page.
(Critical voices in art, theory and culture—
ISSN 1025-9325)
1. Choreography 2. Modern Dance
3.Choreography—Philosophy
4. Modern dance—Philosophy
5. Dance criticism—Philosophy
I. Alexander, Elena, 1944—II. Dunn, Douglas
792.8'2

ISBN 90-5701-082-8

contents

introduction
to the series

CRITICAL VOICES IN ART, THEORY AND
Culture is a response to the changing
perspectives that have resulted from
the continuing application of structural
and poststructural methodologies and
interpretations to the cultural sphere. From the ongoing processes of deconstruction and reorganization of the traditional canon, new forms of speculative,
intellectual inquiry and academic practices have emerged which are premised
on the realization that insights into differing aspects of the disciplines that make
up this realm are best provided by an interdisciplinary approach that follows a
discursive rather than a dialectic model.

In recognition of these changes, and of the view that the histories and
practices that form our present circumstances are in turn transformed by the
social, economic, and political requirements of our lives, this series will publish
not only those authors who already are prominent in their field, or those who
are now emerging—but also those writers who had previously been acknowledged, then passed over, only now to become relevant once more. This multi-
generational approach will give many writers an opportunity to analyze and
reevaluate the position of those thinkers who have influenced their own prac-

tices, or to present responses to the themes and writings that are significant to their own research.

In emphasizing dialogue, self-reflective critiques, and exegesis, the Critical Voices series not only acknowledges the deterritorialized nature of our present intellectual environment, but also extends the challenge to the traditional supremacy of the authorial voice by literally relocating it within a discursive network. This approach to text breaks with the current practice of speaking of multiplicity, while continuing to construct a singularly linear vision of discourse that retains the characteristics of dialectics. In an age when subjects are conceived of as acting upon one another, each within the context of its own history and without contradiction, the ideal of a totalizing system does not seem to suffice. I have come to realize that the near collapse of the endeavor to produce homogeneous terms, practices, and histories—once thought to be an essential aspect of defining the practices of art, theory, and culture—reopened each of these subjects to new interpretations and methods.

My intent as editor of Critical Voices in Art, Theory and Culture is to make available to our readers heterogeneous texts that provide a view that looks ahead to new and differing approaches, and back toward those views that make the dialogues and debates developing within the areas of cultural studies, art history, and critical theory possible and necessary. In this manner we hope to contribute to the expanding map not only of the borderlands of modernism, but also of those newly opened territories now identified with postmodernism.

Saul Ostrow

foreword

jill johnston

I. Closet Criticism

ART ALONE IS NOT A TRUTH-TELLING medium. We have to "read" it to find out what it says. It tends to consist of the same assumptions we as audience bring to the work. Two essential assumptive discourses inhere in every work of art: the language of a particular medium (its aesthetic) as it has evolved to bear on its expressions; and the language of the culture at large, similarly as it impacts art through time and change. Underlying every work is an understood aesthetic/cultural contract—twin conditions that have formed an obedient, unquestioning base for traditional criticism, past and present.

At present, a trend of subversive criticism, ushered in by the revolutionary movements of the 1960s, exists concurrently with the dutiful establishment commentary. The latter, addicted to surface assessments of work, ignoring premises upon which its evaluations rest, has been under assault by feminists, African American analysts, deconstructionists and semioticians—all the code busters—since the seventies. Call the new criticism Closet Criticism. It gets into the closets of narrative and surface, undermining, corrupting the words, sounds, gestures, or movement vocabulary, and formalist policies we take for granted. It resonates with the "closet" of gay and lesbian politics—the only cultural use of the term describing identities hidden from view. It points to the private realm behind the public facade of art. It seeks *reasons* for what we are looking at. Closets are dark places; they hold ulterior motives, secret identities, concealed histories, unconscious strivings, scorned feelings, crimes of shame, arcane intentions, aces in holes, classified information—the skeletons of our past, which we clothe with aesthetics and the language of class, of uniformities and majorities.

Closet Criticism at its best conflates or collapses the private and public spheres. The personal is not truly political—to paraphrase a slogan and war cry of seventies feminists—until the personal or domestic arena is recognized as equally important for change as the state. Looking outward, to the state or culture, to the coercive forces of society that act on our lives and impress our work, Closet Criticism examines all the assumptions of class, gender, sexual orientation, race, ethnicity, religion and age that nourish and power work; it exposes the prejudices that lie hidden within texts and surfaces. A meaningful order, or *nomos*, has been imposed on the discrete experiences and meanings of individuals. An art and criticism that exposes this order makes society liable for the losses in authentic feeling and personal validation resulting from uniform, unquestioned codes.

Looking inward, Closet Criticism creates a critical atmosphere in which the lives of the artists are brought out of the shame of the noncreative, the realm of all closets, where lives are considered unimportant, chaotic, embarrassingly different because private, subject to forces beyond individual control, happily transcended or at least momentarily forgotten in the great enterprises of art. By various methods of inquiry, critics can bring the lives of both living and dead artists into clear apposition with their work. Simple data is available: the givens of gender, race, class, generation; dates of important events in both the lives and careers; dates associated with names of people and works, with the plots of both, and the locations and backgrounds of principals. Meaningful coincidences can be invoked to enliven connections.

Closet Criticism forces the formerly autonomous, incorruptible art object, bereft of information outside itself, virtually a freak of culture, into the open, turning it into a fugitive from truth. The heterosexist discourse that inheres in it, synonymous with patriarchy, is made accountable for the exclusive practices it encourages. And for the censorship it imposes on minority work. And for the self-censorship inhering where it (often overwhelmingly) exists in minority work itself. Art's biographical backgrounds are disclosed (both the genetics of the art medium and the lives of the artists themselves), dictating the revelation that the victims of its prohibitions have not been personally responsible for their obscurity or lack of recognition. Works of art should serve the community, not just the already informed—the cognescenti of a heroized medium, the narrow interests of art markets. Art and criticism should inform the culture at large of its potential for change, its possibility of expanding the cultural language to embrace all aesthetic discourses as equally valid.

Closet Criticism can help move us toward the ideal posthistorical state, in which all "readable" or assumptive texts, scores, choreography and pictures are questioned, in which government and art can be seen as co-dependents or partners in crimes of appearance.

II.

In *Footnotes: Six Choreographers Inscribe the Page*, Elena Alexander has taken the unique step of asking six choreographers to approach the task of writing, not as an illustration of their respective choreographic processes or principles, but as an act in itself. That all six—Douglas Dunn, Marjorie Gamso, Ishmael Houston-Jones, Kenneth King, Yvonne Meier, and Sarah Skaggs—acknowledge their role as choreographers and dancers comes as no surprise. What is surprising and refreshing is the range and complexity of their responses. This is not a book about the specifics of how one goes about making a dance; it is rather, how and what six individuals, whose chosen art form is dance-making, think about that activity in a broader and deeper sense.

Alexander's request to her choreographers to participate had no strings attached; she gave them freedom to write whatever they wanted. With their playfulness, Dunn, Gamso, and King show a kind of dancing on the page, a lively disregard for writerly conventions, inverting the idea of "dancing [as] writing in space," as King writes in his notably dense, intellectually highwired essay. Houston-Jones, who often uses live text in his work, and whose writing, both on dance and other subjects, has often been published, brings us along into one workshop and two perfomances, situating all within an ethical, though never moralistic, framework. Meier and Skaggs, the least text oriented in their approach to dance making, take the opportunity to discuss specific projects, and to inform us of the place their work occupies in a larger political/cultural landscape. All six made good on Alexander's nondirective invitation, providing a spirited, unpredictable mix-and-match—an engaging challenge left to the reader, as final participant, to consider.

Footnotes is choreographed, in a sense, as well as written. In Part I, called "Context," Alexander's voice is "offstage," in the wings, as she inscribes quotes by the choreographers, one by one, among a number of other poets and writers, including journalists. In this giant composite text, the choreographers are acknowledged as writers, their voices indistinguishable from the others, although identifiable in the "(Foot)notes" that follow, along with those of the other authors among whom they are mingled. "Context" is a creative, appropriative "collage" by Alexander, brimming with brief descriptions of space and movement, theories of art and dance, autobiographical snippets, cultural criticism, political sarcasm, comments on the American character, metaphorical interfacing, mythological allusions, dramatic exclamation, semiotic head-of-the-pin "dancing" and much more.

In Part II, her "Exegetical Romp," Alexander writes in her own voice—a "solo," a passionate discussion that reads, at times, like a prose poem. Here she spools out her thoughts on postmodern dance, and the attitudes toward it, and other art forms in general. Alexander, unlike many of her peers, doesn't think or pretend that art is nothing special; she sees it as important work, both historically and in the present. She refuses the cynic's view. Parsing what she calls "the tripartite funding structure," she details the difficulties faced by individual artists and small organizations in today's corporately-influenced climate. She manages throughout her essay to inform as well as inspire.

In Part III, "Text," the writing of the six choreographers quoted earlier in "Context" is presented in full, with Alexander performing a kind of entr'acte, a commentary on each choreographer's essay. Her antiphonal response is in three parts, using the idea of the mirror as a subtle, appropriate conceit for the ostensible subject of choreography and dance. "Image," her reading of the underlying meaning of each choreographer's text, rendered in a single paragraph, is impressionistic, allegorical. In "Reflection" she analyzes each text, revealing keen and sympathetic reflexes to the writings of the choreographers—especially helpful for the reader in cases where the manuscripts are more complex. Lastly, in "Afterimage," Alexander sketches remembered moments in which she saw each of the choreographers perform, and which remained with her, fixed and filmic.

Footnotes: Six Choreographers Inscribe the Page is a unique work: experimental, thoughtful, generous—a crossover book for choreographers, dancers, critics, writers, and readers receptive to a good, multifaceted and layered read.

acknowledgments

Elena Alexander wishes to express her gratitude to each of the six choreographers for their spirited participation. Thanks are also due the following: Ruel Espejo for her assistance throughout, Claudia Steinberg for her translation of Yvonne Meier's text, Saul Ostrow for asking, Quitman Marshall, Frazier Russell, and Eileen Tabios for looking and listening, and Alan Uglow for faith and goodwill overall.

Douglas Dunn would like to thank Elena Alexander for the opportunity and stimulus to write, and to write freely, Anne Waldman for her encouragement and criticism, and Grazia Della-Terza for her support and enthusiasm.

Ishmael Houston-Jones's work has previously been published, in part, in *Contact Quarterly* ("Notes on the Politics of Dancing," winter/spring issue 1996), *FARM* ("The End of Everything," 1990), *Caught in the Act* ("The End of Everything," 1996), and *Out of Character* ("Score for D E A D" 1996). Thanks to Lisa Nelson, Nancy Stark Smith, Mark Russell, and Hudson.

part
one

CONTEXT

IN *THE TASK OF THE TRANSLATOR,* Walter Benjamin stated: "Languages are not strangers to one another, but are, a priori and apart from all historical relationships, interrelated in what they want to express.... The task ... consists in finding that intended effect ... upon the language into which he is translating which produces in it the echo of the original." He goes on to quote Stéphane Mallarmé: "The imperfection of languages consists in their plurality, the supreme one is lacking: thinking is writing without accessories or even whispering, the immortal word still remains silent; the diversity of idioms on earth prevents everybody from uttering the words which otherwise, at one single stroke, would materialize as truth." Benjamin and Mallarmé were speaking quite specifically of writing, but their words have application to the involvement of six choreographers in a textual project. The making of any work of art in any form manifests intention; the reasons why one form is chosen over another are myriad, and though interesting, not the object under scrutiny in *Footnotes*.

The figurative leap taken by Douglas Dunn, Marjorie Gamso, Ishmael Houston-Jones, Kenneth King, Yvonne Meier, and Sarah Skaggs from the medium of choreography into written text constitutes a form of translation. Part I, "Context," inscribes the six within and among other writers, poets, and journalists as ensemble, fabrication, poem.

context

My dessicated formulae are translated into palpable workings of the senses, abuzz with aberrant life, and at once I recognize the flaw in one of my earliest equations compounded a dozen pages on by a further error, and later still, I note a third lapse that, by the merest chance, reconciles the former two, and since — this broken logic to the contrary — my theorem nonetheless holds, I am tempted to leave the manuscript unchanged in homage to the persistence of corruption and the happenstance of rectitude.

—Eric Darton, *Free City*

I

THE LYRICAL nature of pure circulation. . . . The direct star-blast from vectors and signals, from the vertical and the spatial. Hey! The whole body changes frequency, picks up signs and signals. . . Dancing. . . riding through space—all space. . . . Dancing. . . beyond what one can know, or what knowing is. . . . I think we deal with other wisdoms, all more real than our own. . . . Sitting in a chair by the window, I see a man go by. . . and I wonder at the precision with which each foot advances, so controlled. . . so sure. I would hope that if the man and I were to trade places, he might think the same of me. . . but I am not at all sure that he would. I walk along, waving my arms and mumbling almost wordlessly, now shortening my steps so as not to interrupt my mumbling, now mumbling more rapidly in time with my steps. . . . Where this basic dull roar of a rhythm comes from is a mystery. In my case, it's all kinds of repetitions in my mind of noises, rocking motions or. . . any phenomenon with which I can associate a sound. On the one hand. . . we have this rhythm . . . on the other. . . we have the "ego," situated within the space of the language . . . no longer rhythm, but sign, word structure, contract, constraint. . . . Only by vying with the agency of limiting and structuring language does rhythm become a contestant—formulating and

transforming. Listen here. I've never played it safe.... Ask my imaginary brother, that waif, that childhood best friend who comes to play dress-up and stick-
up and jacks and Pick-Up-Sticks.... Or form a Piss Club where we all go in the
bushes and peek at each other's sex. Pop-gunning the street like crows. Not
knowing what to do.... In kindergarten I had the lead as a farmer in a musical production and had to sing! It's a hazy memory and must have been dreadful! ... A few
years later I would have repetitive dreams that my bed was on that stage! An endless and flooded dreamland, lying low, cross-and wheel-studded like a tick-tack-
toe. At the right, ancillary, "Mary" 's close and blue. Which Mary? Aunt Mary?
Tall Mary Stearns I knew? . . . A high *vox humana* somewhere wails: *The gray
horse needs shoeing! It's always the same! What are you doing, there, beyond the
frame?* ... One sees symbolic transactions of movement phenomena in a... continuum extending the kinetics and somatics of movement before and after form
per se, as dreams break the bonds and bounds of reality and perception.
Something like living occurs, a movement/Out of dream into its codification....

2

SIDERATION. Star-blasted, horizontally by the car, altitudinally by the plane . . .
by television. . . . Glorify it how one will, the contents of television are proof
against even the most eloquent stylist's gifts.... [I]t simply will not do to treat
television as a mirror, a reflection of our culture, refusing the possibility that
programming may exert a significant—and debilitating—effect on the life of
our times. I'm surprised at how little invective is directed at the corporate octopus... behind every wall plug. Can it be that a critic... really thinks that the tube
is a thing we turn to in order to see the world rather than a force that significantly
shapes the world... that the medium shows us who we are rather than what a
group of mammoth corporations thinks we'll agree to pretend we are? ... [T]he
fairy tale world of America is more of a dreamed up social life with the kings and
saints of big business.... Jennifer Goodale, manager of cultural programs for the
Philip Morris Companies, [when] asked about scant corporate support for [a
well-known, not-for-profit, photography publisher] said, "We're not in the business of giving away money," to keep an operation afloat. Nonetheless, Philip
Morris is backing a... book [put out by the same publishers] on the dancer and
choreographer Merce Cunningham. "We've been a backer of Merce since 1983,
so this was a wonderful extension of our support," she said. "But it is something

we would not do often because, frankly, companies want something back in terms of marketing visibility. That's the reality."

If you set out afresh the sum to which you attach value and of which you take account

If you were an airman and, without quibbling, flew your arc . . . set the controls for the heart of the sun.

[F]avorably disposed viewers, too, want to fly. . . . They, too, want to transcend the clouds and have a place in the sun. Sheltered by this dazzling light, the semiotician carries on his survey on this side of blindness, in the opaque night of the form he is to illuminate.

[H]ere there is only torment, because. . . you cannot find the right word and solve the problems of the world.

You only solve the equation which the world also is.

Admit that you are merely living in a country furnished by the ancients, that your views are only rented, the pictures of your world hired. Admit that when you really pay . . . you do so only beyond the barrier, when you have said farewell to everything that is so dear to you—to landing places, flying-bases, and only from there do you embark upon your own path. . . . The actions are specific. We had to hike up a mountain. It took something like eight hours. It was completely awful. Then, it was always the question of whether we were going to the restaurant on top of the mountain or not. My parents would never want to go. They brought sandwiches with them; that's what they wanted to eat. I hated it. I couldn't find the food I liked. If I had found it, believe me, I should have made no fuss and stuffed myself like you or anyone else.

Something has innocently changed. *Physical* appearances. . . belonged to solid bodies. Now appearances are volatile. . . mirages; refractions not of light but of appetite, in fact a single appetite, the appetite for more. . . . Oddly, considering the physical implications of the notion of appetite —the existent, the body, disappears. We live within a spectacle of empty clothes and unworn masks. Consider any newsreader on any television channel in any country. These speakers are the mechanical epitome of the *disembodied*. It took the system many years to invent them and to teach them to talk as they do. Then it dawned. I was being silly and old-fashioned. Geography does not matter. . . . When you are king of cyberspace, where you are in relation to your subjects is immaterial. It is the message that counts and how many people you reach. The only drawback to this geography-defying approach is the excess baggage charges—all that satellite and video gear tends to be a bit heavy. . . . Chairman Bill is trying to get his message out to more people than ever before. In his case, the medium really is the message because his theme is always the bright and wonderful world that awaits us when PCs are ubiquitous and easy to use. "Information at Your Fingertips," he calls this vision, or IAYF for people who understand only acronyms. For the last twenty years neither matter nor space nor time has been what it was from time immemorial. We must expect great innovations to transform the entire technique of the arts, thereby affecting artistic invention itself and perhaps even bringing about an amazing change in our very notion of art. No bodies and no Necessity— for Necessity is the condition of the existent. It is what makes reality real. And the system's mythology requires only the not-yet-real, the virtual, the next purchase. This produces in the spectator not, as claimed, a sense of freedom (the so-called freedom of choice) but a profound isolation. There is a time... when the operation of the machine becomes so odious, makes you so sick at heart, that you can't take part; and you've got to put your bodies upon the gears and upon the wheels, upon the levers, upon all the apparatus and you've got to make it stop. And you've got to indicate to the people who run it, to the people who own it, that unless you're free, the machine will be prevented from working at all. The body does not experience the world the same way consciousness does: the gap between these two ways of "processing" experiences punctuates the formation of the unconscious. The function of... analysis... is to repair this join, to find a way to suture the body into time's order. If the body is not, a priori, in time, then dance can be said to be the elaboration of possible temporalities for the body that are interpreted in movement.... Dance frames the body performing movement in time and space... *consciously*.... I think that was why I started doing contact improvisation... The audience is made privy to the... creative process: hierarchies that remove the performer from the spectator are undercut. Also, in a group improvisation, you have to be able to dance with anybody. And that, I thought, was heavily political... moving together, going together to one place... not one teacher or one better than the other, but *together*.

3

AMERICANS are a true utopian society... in their ignorance of the evil genius of things. You have to be utopian to think that in a human order, of whatever nature, things can be... plain and straightforward.... All other societies contain within them some heresy or other, some dissidence, some kind of suspicion... the superstitious belief in a force of evil and the possible control of that force by magic, a belief in the power of appearances. For the moment, I am thinking about… a tale… of… decadence and deceit with a hint of the supernatural: No colours except green and black the walls are green the sky is black (there is no roof) the stars are green the Widow is green but her hair is black as black. When dancing on the right foot, the first movement is a slight hop with the right foot, then the left foot is raised and brought down with a backward scrape along the ground. … The Widow's arm is long as death its skin is green the fingernails are long and sharp and black. Must you kill what you can? I widow redo my life scratch out lies   lie buried inside   the house all the time   sorrows. … There is only one thing I want to do today, and only you can give it to me. It stands at my window, big as the sky. It breathes from my sheets, the cold dead centre   where spilt lives congeal and stiffen to history. This otherness, this "Not-being-us" is all there is to look at in the mirror, though no one can say how it came to be this way. "The haters have gotten slicker. …" Our efforts are like those of the Trojans. We think that with resolution and daring, we will alter the downdrag of destiny. … But when the great crisis comes, our daring and our resolution vanish; our soul is agitated, paralyzed. … The memories and… feelings of our own days weep. Priam and Hecuba weep bitterly for us. [T]he weapon dance… which in Greece was called the *pyrrhiché*… was justly regarded as a real preparation for serious warfare. There is an absolute need to make peace… not for guilt and atonement but for life itself.   Neighbors, the old woman who knows you   turns over in me   and I wake up   another country.   [W]e pass   through   one   another   like   blowing   snow,   all   of   us,   all. I am searching for words to describe… feverish and futile, hilarious and hysterical efforts. … [I]t is necessary to raise certain questions for consideration by anyone who wishes to put the pieces… back together again. The… task hinges on how the terms 'lost' and 'found' are understood. I am searching—searching through my handbag … my bookshelf … my childhood memories—searching everywhere for words to describe the way movement phrases… begin to change. … [U]se it as a signal to bring your attention very close. [G]ive some attention to the analogy between understanding dance and understanding language. Sociologist Erving Goffman's observations about how we organize experience and "manage impressions" are telling. … As in the theater, sometimes we are "onstage," with all the conventions and limitations that implies. Sometimes we are "offstage"—able to relax from the strenuous demands of the role. "[K]eying" of a particular activity… is a conscious transformation of that activity into something quite different, although modeled on the original activity. Examples of keyings are fantasies, daydreams. . . and. . . certain sports (imitating combat but different in crucial ways); ceremonies such as weddings . . . re-doings such as rehearsals. . . . It seems no accident that the work of a sociologist should parallel the investigations of. . . contemporary performance. . . . WHEN ONE DOES NOT RESEMBLE WHAT THEY ARE SUPPOSED TO BE   When concave insight is mastermind of the spiritual, the search goes on internally. . .   —soon we will wonder, not wait. . . for answers, but investigate   the chase for the private life goes on while the public life escalates. . . [T]he pain. . . comes from the tiresome process of re-devaluation. . . perhaps it is the moral issue of the unsaid. . . perhaps it is the illicit nature of possibility. . . . If you can lift up a phone and find the desired one at home, then you have eliminated even the memory of a long walk through error and distraction to get to the object of your desires. However, mythic responses to one's helpless subjection to time and space—to being lost and found—still exist in the night and dreams just as they exist in art, poetry, music. Andrei Tarkovsky said that art should remind us why life is worth living. . . .

4

A BLUE-GREEN lorry with gleaming chromework is going down Seventh Avenue in the early morning sun, just after a snowfall. It bears on its sides, in gold metallic lettering, the words 'Mystic Transportation.' [W]hat I see on the street I watch out stay inside walk don't walk enough not to get hit plus cue off others for less formal limits shall I jaywalk here do cabs press hard there yes they turn threateningly into my crosswalking but this grid to go by only background not the high-tech big-town homecity night-lit multifaceted treasure we eyeballers came for. . . . How funny you are today New York like Ginger Rogers in *Swingtime* and St. Bridget's steeple leaning a little to the left. . . and even the traffic halt so thick is a way for people to rub up against each other and when their surgical appliances lock they stay together for the rest of the day (what a day). . . and the park's full of dancers and their tights and shoes in little bags. . . . I walked up Wooster toward Houston, past the metal doors of the loft buildings. Reaching Prince, I looked across the corner at FOOD, which. . . had been started by artists to have someplace to eat in the wilderness of SoHo, and was now thronged with art tourists. You try to avoid judgments, but once you let a few out you seem freed to state more clearly your own ideals and direction. Take the crudest, most obvious example. You buy yourself a pair of boots. What do you know about them? That they suit you or they don't, that you like them or you don't. That they were bought in a certain shop. . . . Can you judge their durability? Their quality? No. Why? Because you're not the bootmaker. . . . It's the same with art. . . exactly the same. You either like it or you don't, it comes across to you or it doesn't. . . . But whether it is good or bad. . . only an expert can say, or one who loves it—or the master craftsman. In judging a world you do not live in, you are simply exceeding your rights. And all the while, I—congenitally dishonest like all artists—try to recoup truth by convincing you of something about some aspect of my artifact. . . orgy of false being life in common brief shames I am not dead to inexistence not irretrievably time will tell it's telling but what a hog's wallow pah not even not even pah brief moments of the lower face. . . . Trying is trying trying not to is trying only not trying is not trying. . . soon unbearable thump on skull long silence vast stretch of time soon unbearable opener arse or capitals if he has lost the thread YOUR LIFE CUNT ABOVE CUNT HERE CUNT as it comes bits and scraps all sorts. . . and to conclude. . . I came out of the subway, Lenox Avenue seemed to career away from me at a drunken angle, and I focused upon the teetering scene with wild, infant's eyes, and my head throbbing.

5

NOW, you can say anything you like about Americans, but they are neither mediocre nor petty-bourgeois. They certainly do not have aristocratic grace, but they have an ease that comes from space, and this makes up for a lack of manners or noble breeding. Vulgar but 'easy.' For those who construct the. . . standards, this must certainly be immensely frustrating. . . . They have power but are unsure. . . . No doubt some individuals and institutions will appear to be reexamining the old standards and offering new ones. . . . However, the issue will not be whether the standards are new or not, but whether they, like the old standards, make denial an official and efficient program. . . . This is a culture which sets up specialized institutes so that people's bodies can come together and touch, and, at the same time, invents pans in which the water *does not touch* the bottom of the pan, which is made of a substance so homogeneous, dry, and artificial that not a single drop sticks to it, just like those bodies intertwined in 'feeling' and therapeutic love, which do not touch—not even for a moment. This is called interface or interaction. I wanted something more multifaceted that would address the more elusive ways in which people perceive others and make assumptions about what those perceptions might mean. I wanted to explore some of the subtle and not-so-subtle ways people act upon those perceptions and assumptions. Distance. What does distance matter;   how does distance work. Can it   even unwind a man, then wind him up again?   Of course it's the principle that counts,   if there's a principle that counts.   What direction is it from?   The same direction. And is   the other data correct?   When the upper lip is raised   the teeth feel cold.   When both lips are gone,   your teeth feel colder.... This man bows to where nothing is; picks up... rope, rolls up the rope, blows away... letters and goes away himself... running down the street past the Palace Hotel. Ripping up the shrubbery. Throwing paving stones. It's a lot like TV. We spent about forty-five minutes splitting apart, regrouping, then splitting apart again. We spent almost as much time afterwards discussing what it all could mean. How the form is developing. What I am saying does not mean that there will henceforth be no form.... It only means that there will be a new form, and that this form will be of such a type that it admits the chaos and does not try to say that the chaos is really something else. It forces one to publicly declare aspects of the self that are taken for granted, or are not often acknowledged (perhaps even to oneself). The most vexing statement has been "I BELIEVE THAT I AM IN THE MORE INTELLIGENT HALF OF THIS...." When I was in India training with my teacher, Minindra-ji, I sat in on many of his interviews with yogis to watch how he taught. After some of the interviews, he would describe which meditation subjects were suitable for different individuals. Once he said, "Oh, yes, this one is suitable for intelligent people, and this one for stupid people." Because of a certain... conditioning, I was offended that anyone would be considered stupid. Isn't it like this? First of all, people use an explanation, a chart... later they, as it were, look it up in the head (by calling it before the inner eye, or the like).... But for our present purpose can't we say "he is writing" and "I am writing" instead of "he understands" and "I understand?" Then we leave the question of experience *completely* out of the game. Also, for instance, the question of private understanding. "Your legs are very beautiful but what are those marks?"

6

UTOPIA *has been achieved here and anti-utopia is being achieved.* Paradise is just paradise. The question of its origin was immediately the question of its end. Its history is *constructed* like the ruin of a monument which basically never existed. It is the history of a ruin, the narrative of a memory which produces the event to be told and which will never have been present. There is no notion more "revolutionary" than this history, but the "revolution" will also have to be changed. But is this really what an achieved utopia looks like? Is this a successful revolution? Yes indeed! What do you expect a successful revolution to look like? It is paradise. *Paradise* . . . challenges our limited concept. . . allowing audience members and performers, over an extended length of time, and in a variety of settings, to both inform and be informed, to create and respond, and ultimately, to begin to approach. . . not only on a thematic level, but through shared, kinetic experience. That same enthusiasm which Americans themselves show for their own success...their own power. So, then, the unique structure of an event, for the. . . act I am speaking of must be an event. It will only receive its status of invention. . . to the extent that this socialization of the invented thing will be protected by a system of *conventions* that will ensure for it at the same time its recording in a common history, its belonging to a culture: to a heritage, a lineage, a pedagogical tradition, a discipline, a chain of generations. The experiments Dancers' Workshop . . . did in the 1960s and '70s with new *forms* of dance led to new *uses* of dance. Dancing outside the confines of the proscenium theater . . . had unexpected results. We researched new uses of dance and movement, and our forms became accessible to more people and began to exist outside the theater and in the daily lives of ordinary people. In the process of stripping away all pretense. . . and. . . engaging the whole person. . . an unexpected synthesis occurred. We were tapping into our own personal stories, and the dances. . . had transformative powers. . . as myths. The words I keep thinking of to describe it come perilously close to current psychotherapeutic clichés: reality of encounter, responsible interaction, truthful response. To put it in a more personal way. . . a glimpse of human behavior that my dreams for a better life are based on—real, complex, constantly in flux, rich, concrete, funny, focused, immediate, specific, intense, serious at times to the point of religiosity, light, diaphanous, silly, and many leveled at any particular moment. Consider what is expected of us by the dynamic of collective conscience and the will to liberty in various circumstances and places. As residents of the United States, we might claim *Leaves of Grass*— or sew together and claim the folk tales and songs with the story of the survival of slavery in them. . . . Every culture has its traditional stories, no matter how diffused they may have become. . . . Each body has its art, precious prescribed pose, that even in passion's droll contortions, waltzes, or push of pain—or when a grief has stabbed or hatred hacked—is its and nothing else's. It is distinctive of any art form that its conventions allow for the possibility of the expression of a conception of life situations. A trip I took to Bali in 1992 was an epiphany . . . I traveled on my bike to villages. . . . The shrines were filled with offerings. . . oranges, lemons, palm leaves, paper cups, fabric, and flowers—items from everyday life, not golden goblets. . . . It was a bustling mixture of commerce. . . socializing, eating, and gambling on cock fights. The mixture of activity boggled the mind. There, dance is a part of everyday life. Dance functions as a model for social order, illustrating their complex cosmology and insuring through the stories in their dances, a balanced society. . . . I will tell you something about stories. They aren't just entertainment. Don't be fooled. Those in the dominant groups devalue stories for different reasons; inundated by texts, perceiving themselves as part of "history," they are confident that their stories will be told for them and they are less likely to understand the crucial significance of personal/communal memory. . . . The Indians tell us . . . The wind is carrying me round the sky   The wind is carrying me round the sky   My body is here in the valley—The wind is carrying me round the sky.   Inside each of us is this small paradise.[1]

[Foot]notes

I

1. **The lyrical . . . the spatial.**
   Jean Baudrillard, *America*, trans. Chris Turner (London: Verso, 1988), 27–28.

   Hey! . . . what knowing is.
   Kenneth King, "Sight & Cipher" [excerpted from "Ideosigns and Isomorphisms"] in *SIGHTLINES AND IDEOSIGNS*, 1994. Manuscript unpublished as of the date of publication of this book.

   I think . . . that he would.
   Robert Creeley, "Fate Tales." In *The Gold Diggers and Others Stories* (New York: Charles Scribner's Sons, 1965), 49.

   I walk along . . . associate a sound.
   Vladimir Mayakovsky, *How Are Verses Made?*, trans. G.M. Hyde (London: J. Cape, 1970), 36–37.

   On the one hand . . . contract, constraint.
   Julia Kristeva, *Desire in Language: A Semiotic Approach to Literature and Art*, ed. Leon S. Roudiez, trans. Thomas Gora, Alice Jardine and Leon S. Roudiez (New York: Columbia University Press, 1980), 28–29.

Only by ... transforming.
Ibid., 29.

Listen here ... what to do.
Anne Sexton, "August 8th." In *Words for Dr. Y*, ed. Linda Grey Sexton (Boston: Houghton Mifflin, 1978), 75.

In kindergarten ... on that stage!
Kenneth King, "Autobiopathy." In *Footnotes* (1992), 122.

An endless ... frame?
Elizabeth Bishop, "Sunday, 4 a.m." In *Elizabeth Bishop, The Complete Poems: 1927–1979* (New York: Farrar, Straus & Giroux, 1995), 129.

One sees ... perception.
King, 114.

Something like ... codification.
John Ashbery, "Self-Portrait in a Convex Mirror." In *Self-Portrait in a Convex Mirror* (New York: Penguin Books, 1975), 73.

2

Sideration ... by television.
Baudrillard, 27.

Glorify it ... plug.
Sven Birkerts, *The New York Times Book Review* (March 2, 1997), 7.

Can it be ... world.
Ibid., 7.

[T]hat the medium ... we are.
Ibid., 7.

The fairy tale world ... big-business.
Ernst Bloch, "The Fairy Tale Moves on Its Own Time." In The Utopian Function of Art and Literature, trans. Jack Zipes and Frank Mecklenburg (Cambridge, MA: MIT Press, 1988), 164.

Jennifer Goodale ... reality.
Anthony Ramirez, *New York Times*, (February 16, 1997), city section, 4.

If you were ... your arc.
Ingeborg Bachmann, "The Thirtieth Year." In *The Thirtieth Year*, trans. Michael Bullock (New York: Holmes & Meier, 1987), 31.

Set the controls ... sun.
Pink Floyd, "Set the Controls for the Heart of the Sun"
Ummagumma, EMI/Harvest STB-338 (1969).

Favorably disposed ... sun.
Bloch, 164.

Sheltered ... illuminate.
Kristeva, 104–105.

[11]ere ... also is.
Bachmann, 30.

Admit ... your own path.
Ibid., 22.

The ... specific.
Yvonne Meier, "The Shining." In *Footnotes*, 143.

We had ... to go.
Yvonne Meier, interview w/Gina Kourlas, *Time Out New York* no. 73, (1997): 62.

They brought ... it.
Yvonne Meier, as told to Elena Alexander, (1997).

I couldn't find ...anyone else.
Franz Kafka, "A Hunger Artist," trans. Willa and Edwin Muir, In *The Complete Stories*, ed. Nahum N. Glatzer (Schocken Books, New York, 1971) 277.

Something has ... as they do.
John Berger, *Tate Art Magazine* 11 (Spring 1997): 40.

Then it dawned ... acronyms.
Andrew North, *The Independent*, London (November 25, 1996), 11.

For the last ... notion of art.
Paul Valery, "The Conquest of Ubiquity." In *Aesthetics*, trans. Ralph Manheim (New York: Pantheon Books, 1964), 225.

No bodies ... profound isolation.
Berger, 40.

There ... working at all.
Mario Savio, quoted by Eric Pace, *New York Times* (November 8, 1996), B38.

The body does not ... time's order.
Peggy Phelan, "Dance and the History of Hysteria." In *Corporealities: Dancing Knowledge, Culture and Power,* ed. Susan Leigh Foster, (London and New York: Routledge, 1996), 91.

If the body ... consciously.
Ibid., 92.

I think . . . improvisation.

Yvonne Meier, in tape recorded conversation with Elena Alexander, November 12, 1996.

The audience . . . anybody.

Sally Banes, "Dancing in Leaner Times." In *Writing Dancing in the Age of Postmodernism* (Hanover, NH: Wesleyan University Press/University Press of New England, 1994), 345–346.

And that . . . together.

Yvonne Meier in tape recorded conversation with Elena Alexander, November 12, 1996.

3

Americans are . . . power of appearances.

Baudrillard, 85.

For the moment . . . supernatural.

Marjorie Gamso, "Cover(t) Stories." In *Footnotes*, 66.

No colours except green . . . black as black.

Salman Rushdie, *Midnight's Children* (New York: Avon Books, 1980), 249.

When dancing . . . along the ground.

Joseph Campbell, *The Masks of God: Primitive Mythology* (Middlesex, England: Penguin, 1976), 366.

The Widow's arm . . . sharp and black.

Rushdie, 249.

Must you kill what you can?

Sylvia Plath, "A Birthday Present." In *Ariel* (New York: Harper & Row, 1961), 44.

I widow . . . all the time sorrows.

Mitsuye Yamada, "Homecoming." In *No More Masks! An Anthology of Twentieth Century American Women Poets*, ed. Florence Howe (New York: Harper Perennial, 1993), 156.

There is only . . . history.

Plath, 44.

This otherness...this way.

John Ashbery, "Self-Portrait in a Convex Mirror." In *Self-Portrait in a Convex Mirror* (New York: Penguin Books, 1975), 81.

"The haters have gotten slicker."

Don Terry, "A Lesson in Hate Intrudes at One School." *New York Times* (May 25, 1996), 8.

Our efforts . . . bitterly for us.
C.P. Cavafy, "The Trojans." In *The Complete Poems of Cavafy*, trans. Rae Dalven, (New York: Harcourt Brace & World, 1961), 14.

The weapon dance . . . serious warfare.
Curt Sachs, *World History of the Dance*, trans. Bessie Schoenberg (New York: Norton, 1937), 239.

There is an absolute . . . life itself.
Amos Oz, edited version of a speech made by Oz, regarding the Peace Prize awarded by German publishers and booksellers, *The Guardian* (October 5, 1992), 21.

Neighbors . . . all of us, all.
Linda Hogan, "Our Houses." In *Cries of the Spirit: A Celebration of Women's Spirituality*, ed. Marilyn Sewell (Boston: Beacon Press, 1991), 223.

I am searching . . . hysterical efforts.
Gamso, 65.

[I]t is necessary . . .understood.
Kenneth Archer and Millicent Hodson, "Ballets Lost and Found: Restoring the Twentieth Century Repetoire." In *Dance History: An Introduction*, eds. Janet Adshead-Lansdale and June Layson (London and New York: Routledge, 1983), 99.

I am searching . . . begin to change.
Gamso, 65.

Use it . . . very close.
Joseph Goldstein, *Insight Meditation: The Practice of Freedom* (Boston and London: Shambala, 1993), 80.

[G]ive some . . . language.
Graham McFee, *Understanding Dance* (London and New York: Routledge, 1992), 112.

Sociologist Erving Goffman's . . . demands of the role.
Sally Banes, *Terpsichore in Sneakers: Post-Modern Dance* (Boston: Houghton Mifflin, 1980), 210.

[K]eying of . . . original activity.
Ibid., 211.

Examples . . . such as rehearsals.
Ibid., 211–212.

It seems no accident ... performance.
Ibid., 212.

When one ... nature of possibility.
Lori Lubeski, "The Unsolicited Identity We Are." In *Children of the Cold War, A Scrapbook, Five Fingers Review 13* (San Francisco: Five Fingers Press, 1994), 180–182.

If you lift ... living.
Fanny Howe, introduction to *Children of the Cold War*, viii.

4

A blue-green lorry ... 'Mystic Transportation'.
Baudrillard, 21.

[W]hat I see ... eyeballers came for.
Douglas Dunn, "I'm Dancing." In *Footnotes*, 45.

How funny ... in little bags.
Frank O'Hara, "Steps." In *Lunch Poems* (San Francisco: City Lights Books, 1964), 56–57.

I walked ... art tourists.
Michael Brownstein, *Self-Reliance* (Minneapolis: Coffee House Press, 1994), 250.

You try to avoid ... direction.
Dunn, 55.

Take the crudest ... your rights.
Maria Tsvetaeva, *Art in the Light of Conscience* (Cambridge, MA: Harvard University Press, 1992), 44.

And all the while ... of my artifact.
Richard Foreman, "How Truth ... Leaps (Stumbles) Across Stage." In *Performing Arts Journal 14* (1981): 92.

[O]rgy of false being ... the lower face.
Samuel Beckett, *How It Is* (New York: Grove Press, 1964), 69.

Trying is ... trying
Dunn, 55.

Soon unbearable ... conclude.
Beckett, 75.

I came ... head throbbing.
Ralph Ellison, *Invisible Man* (New York and London: Penguin, 1952), 204.

5

Now, you can say . . . Vulgar but 'easy'.
Baudrillard, 94.

For those who construct . . . efficient program.
John Yau, *In the Realm of Appearances: The Art of Andy Warhol*
(Hopewell, NJ: The Ecco Press, 1993), 55.

This is . . . interface or interaction.
Baudrillard, 32.

I wanted . . . perceptions and assumptions.
Ishmael Houston-Jones, "A Dance of Identity: Notes on The Politics
of Dancing." In *Footnotes,* 99.

Distance . . . that counts.
Hans Favery, *Against the Forgetting,* trans. Francis R. Jones (London:
Anvil Press Poetry, 1994), 40.

What direction . . . correct?
Ibid., 41.

When the upper . . . teeth feel colder.
Ibid., 43.

This man . . . goes away himself.
Ibid., 31.

[R]unning . . . like T.V.
Ishmael Houston-Jones, "The Annotated *End of Everything*." In *Footnotes,* 92.

We spent . . . developing.
Houston-Jones, "A Dance," 98.

What I am . . . is really something else.
Deirdre Bair, *Samuel Beckett* (London: Picador/Pan Books, 1980), 442.

It forces . . . oneself).
Houston-Jones, "A Dance," 100.

The most vexing...OF THIS.
Houston-Jones, "A Dance," 101.

When I was in India . . . considered stupid.
Goldstein, 6.

Isn't it like this? . . . or the like).
Ludwig Wittgenstein, *Philosophical Grammar,* ed. Rush Rhees, trans.
Anthony Kenny (Berkeley and Los Angeles: University of California
Press, 1974), 85.

But for our present purpose . . . private understanding.
Ibid., 83–84.

Your . . . marks?
Houston-Jones, "The Annotated *End,*" 94.

6

Utopia . . . achieved.
Baudrillard, 97.

Paradise . . . paradise.
Ibid., 98.

The question of its origin . . . to be changed.
Jacques Derrida, "This Strange Institution Called Literature." In *Acts of Literature*, ed. Derek Attridge trans. Geoffrey Bennington and Rachel Bowlby, edited transcript of interview, Lagua Beach, California, 1989 (London and New York: Routledge, 1992), 42.

But . . . it is paradise.
Baudrillard, 98.

Paradise challenges . . . experience.
Sarah Skaggs, "Paradise Remixed." In *Footnotes*, 154–155.

That same . . . power.
Baudrillard, 98.

So then...chain of generations.
Source unknown; this was among E. Alexander's notes, without citation information.

The experiments . . . results.
Anna Halperin, preface to *Moving Toward Life: Five Decades of Transformational Dance*, ed. Rachael Kaplan (Hanover, NH: Wesleyan University Press, 1995), xi.

[W]e researched . . . ordinary people.
Ibid., xi.

In the process . . . synthesis occurred.
Ibid., xii.

We were tapping . . . powers . . . as myths.
Ibid., xii.

The words . . . particular moment.
Yvonne Rainer, *Work 1961–73* (Halifax: The Press of the Nova Scotia College of Art and Design; New York: New York University Press, 1974), 148.

Consider what is expected . . . places.
Nadine Gordimer, *The Essential Gesture: Writing, Politics and Places*,
ed. Stephen Clingman (London: Penguin, 1989), 288.

As residents . . . slavery in them.
Adrienne Rich (citing Suzanne Gardiner), *What is Found There:
Notebooks on Poetry and Politics* (New York: Norton, 1993), 63.

Every culture . . . become.
Lucy Lippard, *Mixed Blessings: New Art in a Multicultural America*
(New York: Pantheon, 1990), 100.

Each body . . . nothing else's.
Gwendolyn Brooks, "Still Do I Keep My Look, My Identity." In *The
Poetry Anthology: 1912–1977*, eds. Daryl Hine and Joseph Parisi
(Boston: Houghton Mifflin, 1978), 242.

It is a distinctive . . . of life situations.
Graham McFee (citing David Best), *Understanding Dance* (London
and New York: Routledge, 1994), 174.

A trip I took . . . balanced society.
Skaggs, 149–150

I will tell you . . . fooled.
Lippard (citing Leslie Marmon Silko), 97.

Those in the dominant . . . personal/communal memory.
Ibid., 100–101.

The Indians tell us . . . round the sky.
Carl Sandburg, "Alice Corbin is Gone." In *The Poetry Anthology,
1912–1977*, 364.

Inside each . . . paradise.
John Kifner, "A Palestinian Version of the Judgment of Solomon."
New York Times (October 16, 1992), A2.

part
two

EXEGETICAL
ROMP

exegetical romp

elena alexander

SHE IS DEEP INSIDE THE MOMENT, hat pulled low over the eyes, torso and stomach convex through arduous arching of the back, weight placed forward on balls of feet and toes as she howls a tone hour after hour and is it art, no, it is not, but it could be if shaped by choreographer or writer who might alter or attain-as-understanding what others ignore or consider merely pitiable or bothersome, this woman standing day after day at a low wall surrounding a bank in a city, making manifest—one might imagine—her connection between corruption and ignorance, the holiness of body and sound, trying to save humanity from its own dumb folly, and do we appreciate her, no, we do not, we think she is plumb crazy, as we rush about our lives, and if we achieve a momentary sense of guilt or what we believe is our own guileless, kindly nature we think she should be removed for her own good and if we are feeling grumpy we think she should JUST GO AWAY, unless we accede to our complicity, acknowledge exploitation as debt, seek her beyond her flesh, observe how we might cozy up to her state of mind. We have to be alert.

Connections. "Everything is connected to everything else." This observation was put forth by a lawyer, Vladimir Ilich Ulyanov, though it was attributed to him as Lenin. Did Lenin dream? Perhaps. "Mother was there, and, later, Father. I kept trying to tell them, 'Everything is ... every *thing* is ...' but I could not finish, could not speak. Then I was flying and I was falling, caught in a tangle of red ribbons, each with an end tied to a seemingly unrelated object covering an expansive murky interior in which there were mountains, plateaus, rivers, as though part of a monumental stage set for a play in which I was to be the star. The objects began turning into people, the people back into objects, the objects into oxen, the oxen into people. It went on like this, all of it transforming, connecting." Something like that. Impossible to know. More probably, it came to him while awake, in the form of a worded intuition or conclusion discovered while thinking, from reading, in talking with others. "Everything is connected to everything else" lacks innocence, in Lenin's case, though not perspicacity, even with its author as out of fashion as the very word, author. In the context in which it was formulated it is assertive, stating that that which we may not readily see can still be said to influence the course of events, and the most seemingly unrelated interests or categories may have an impact on other areas which, if not immediately obvious, prove unassailable given a large enough scope or, in some cases, a long enough rope. It might also be argued that once the connections are pointed out, a political consensus ensues as to what is meant by reality. With a different adjustment in point of view, we can observe each moment within an ever-changing continuum, finding ourselves in accord with Eastern spiritual and philosophical precepts. As still another countervailing strategy or idea, others may stress that there are no underlying connections, but that all is random and unrelated, an infinite number of subjective constructs to which meaning or value is attached by unconscious, ineluctable habit or conditioning. Styles change, whether hem lengths or ideas. Emphases shift. There are arbiters of fashion. We must pay attention.

(The construct-of-an-ever-changing-I stops to consider a metaphor: Everything written thus far, everything about to follow, is a dive into the language pool. You might say swan dive, cannonball, belly flop. Thoughts arrive that describe visual images, denote a state of mind or a physical sensation in the solar plexus, and they are written down, though this style of self-conscious writing quickly becomes claustrophobic, precious. The ostensibly-conscious, writerly-I—with all of the influences that connect everything to everything else, or an I that shifts while an It remains eternal, or another, in which subterranean, vague and random chunks float, like debris in space—return to my pool-and-dive metaphor. Do I propel myself into the empty blue sky from a great height or simply let go, toppling in from a low, safe ledge? The preceding sentence is both language in the act of making itself, and imagined choreographed actions an actual body might perform.)

We can recontextualize this idea of connections in the light of technology. Bill Gates, chairman of Microsoft, might employ Lenin's obser-vation as a marketing gambit, much as an advertising firm dreamed up the slogan, "Reach out and touch someone" for AT&T, since updated to "It's all within your reach." "Everything is connected to everything else." Seems it should be a techno-adman's dream. There are violent dreams, peaceful dreams. Fifty-two wrathful deities, forty-eight peaceful, in the Tibetan Buddhist pantheon. This is a striking statistic. There are those who say they do not remember their dreams. To not recall a dream is to not recount a dream. We tend to see this as repression. Perhaps it is a profound visualization, a silent film, a deep dance. All image, no language, meant to remain unspoken. Logically impossible to imagine.

Have all choreographers had at least one flying dream they can describe in detailed analogy? Dance, the concrete dream. Can a dream be con-crete? A wind, invisible, can tear up trees, houses, kill cows and humans. Do all choreographers remember their dreams, those random juxtapositions and occurrences, shorn of value judgments, where we apply different criteria to what we mean by a sequence of events, finding that that logic means poetry?

(More metaphor: The fingertips of one hand stretch up to touch the self-luminous, celestial blue-white body of a star, while the fingertips of the other rub the curled, rough surface of a dried starfish before the whole body encounters the fish that grants three wishes. Language in the act of describing actions that the choreographed body cannot literally actualize, but which the mind can imagine and reveal in written form.)

The choreographer imagines the organs within the body, the space within a room, the length of a limb, the lordotic mating posture of rats, the courtship dance of cranes, the body as object and ardor falling hard into love or against the floor, over and over only to stand again, imagines the focus of eyes as the focal point of meaning, the skipping of feet or stomp of a foot, the curve of a long, thin pencil-line of torso, the morsel of gesture in lifting the pinkie, the entire body flying through space, a momentous if momentary respite from gravity before being caught by another, or by surprise if an expected body is not there to catch the flying one. Everything connected to everything else. Flesh to bones to organs, tissues, cells. Femur to ephemera: the bones will disappear within a finite cycle or span. Tibia to Tennilleo or Tbilisi: the bones' forebears, regardless of when or where the body is dancing, could be from Georgia in the south of what is the U.S., or what was the U.S.S.R.

Connections. Economics to art-making. The dissipation of the tripartite structure—government, foundations, corporations—which, though fragile and insufficient, formed the immediate constituents of an arts-funding program, has seen the breaking off of one corner of this configuration, the dissolution of a federal arts budget and the diminution of many state budgets. It was always tacitly understood by those who depended upon its existence in order to continue their own work—and choreographers were in the first rank here—that the federal arts budget, even at its most extensive, was an absurdly small percentage of the federal budget overall. For all the arts, and certainly for dance, two factors prevailed in relation to federal funds: (1) every dollar counted, and dollars were ceded in amounts which, though not enough on their own, were crucial, and (2) those who received grants were given, in lieu of sufficient hard cash, that sub rosa, Realpolitik, all-important, here's-what-justified-arts'-bureaucrats'-weekly-paychecks, an *imprimatur*. That imprimatur meant—as does USDA to beef—that a particular piece of art, in whatever form, was "Gov't Apprv'd". It signaled to other funders within foundations and corporations - as well as to individual patrons outside those structures - that this was work they, too, might think seriously about supporting, thus supplying the remaining funds making it possible for the recipients to make their work and if possible, though rare, to live without having to hold down one or more jobs, in addition to that of art-making. This concept—having money to live on from the making of art—is hard to come by in the United States. The puritan ethic under which we continue to live and struggle—no matter how many times it is pointed out—already perceives art-making as play and pleasure, which it is, and refuses to support such a notion. What this national superego does not apprehend is that art-making is also a serious, and seriously engaging, form of work in which *commitment* and *discipline*—two puritan qualities if ever there were—are paramount. Choreographers and dancers are forced to acknowledge and practice both, or they cannot make or perform dances. This is tautological; it is also true. Two other thoughts in regard to the destruction of a federal arts budget: In structural terms, the process was open to all and was decided by eliminative rounds done by peer panel review; it was not perfect, but it endeavored to remain fair, and more often than not, succeeded. Second, *individual artists* were encouraged to apply because there was such a category; shamefully, it was excised before the agency waned to its present state. The federal arts budget went from inadequate to minuscule to, as of this writing, virtually none. Artists themselves operate from a place of fear; it is not a position offering freedom of movement. What current attitudes and policy reveal is a willingness to leave decisions for the fate of the arts in unfriendly hands. These hands construct a formidable architecture, twin towers of power and control. In language, there is the much-discussed death of the author, the *authority*. This discourse seems to have escaped scrutiny in regard to arts funding: who decides who gets what, and how much. Or perhaps it has not yet begun in earnest.

When federal funding for the arts was discredited, leaving individual artists and small organizations foundering, private foundations were unable to pick up all the slack. Foundations, not being subject to the baiting of hooks to catch red herrings, do not have to justify their decisions to taxpayers—who are led to believe that artists are parading around naked on Easy Street, taking huge chunks out of the deficit-encumbered budget while fraying the moral fiber of the country—but they do have boards of directors and bylaws. A substantial number of these foundations are administered by those whose goals and commitment share common cause with those they support, and they remain an

individual artist's or small organization's best hope, short of the much imagined—though usually chimerical—substantial endowment or, in rare cases,
large inheritance. Even sympathetic foundations cannot be expected to pick up
the entire shortfall left by the gap in federal support. On occasion, foundations
suffer from investment strategies gone awry, or other reversals of fortune leading to diminished funds—a diminution which can exponentially affect those
they might otherwise wish to support. There are also foundations that have followed the trend toward giving larger amounts to fewer numbers, which helps
lend credence to the tried-and-true, or *masterpiece,* theory, the last idea that
needs further publicity. One small slip of a consonant, and we are left with
mater, mother. This is striking: language in its associative mode, creating room
for the female gender to make the same mistake.

What about the third corner of the funding structure, corpora-
tions? From all indications, it appears that this is not a solution to a responsible
and realistic funding program for dance, or for any of the arts over the long haul.
Individual choreographers, especially the younger or the more experimental, do
not count in corporate boardrooms. Marketing strategies and packaging are
what count in boardrooms. National recognition counts. Largesse for the
largest. High yield on an investment. Bang   for   the   buck. We might
consider the economy of freedom in this Age of Commerce, the
corporate tail wagging the art dog. Corporate logos plastered on costumes?
Perhaps. It's an idea to contemplate. Just the way the athletes do it. Don't get me
wrong—I love/d sports. It's the logos I detest. Corporations get much more in
the way of whitewashed image than they give in the way of dollars. They are
ready to jettison arts funding at the first whiff of perceived difficulty or scandal, although part of the attraction is that the arts may come with a cachet of
respectability *and* an aura of naughtiness. It is disheartening to see dance working so hard at trying to package itself as though it had substance, was anything
but what it is: impermanence personified. Who knows what is exciting! fabu-
lous! even revelatory!? When everyone lies, everyone loses.

"Dance eats money." This observation was put forth by a choreographer and dancer, Arnie Zane. Mr. Zane is no longer alive in the flesh, but his
observation lands on a page and remains; we can consider it, discuss it with others, dream about it, go back and reflect on it, play around with the image and its

possible meanings and implications. "Dance eats money." Surely a metaphor, not to be taken literally, because another logical impossibility. What did Mr. Zane mean? It would appear that by "eats money," he did not mean biting, chewing, and swallowing as a human might, a bit at a time, but more like the glowing receptacle on an old steam engine consuming coal as fast as a man could shovel it in in order to create the energy to pull or push a line of railroad cars, or a blast furnace absorbing infusions of air so as to produce the intense heat needed for smelting. And if we do take humans as an example, we must eat daily to convert the food-as-fuel into energy for survival. If not, then we suffer accordingly and eventually die. It's basic and common, though not to be easily dismissed. The steam created by stoking a furnace transforms into smoke and disappears. How can we be asked to support something as stubbornly and relentlessly illusory as dance, with its constant need for stoking, so that all its 'moving parts' can function, while its results disappear like smoke? What kind of snake oil is this? Can't someone just dance around a room, unencumbered by specific costumes, lights, props, and sets? Certainly, and someone has—many have. But what of all the others? No. Dance eats money.

Do extreme marketing strategies in regard to stay-at-home technology place additional stress on already strained art forms that depend on live presentation? Yes, they do. Was this also true of real estate concerns in the 1980s buying up loft spaces in lower Manhattan and selling them at exorbitant prices? Yes, it was. The arts help sell neighborhoods, make them desirable. Has either been part of a plot to further undermine or put the squeeze on dance and the other arts? No, they have not. Does life contain ironies? Yes. Lack of attention to larger matters—to connections—is a form of harmful ignorance, even if done without malice. That's why there is a category of crime called manslaughter. Connections everywhere, or from a different point of view, only connect. Whichever you choose, however you do it, observe carefully; the dots will begin to form a picture.

Information, opinion, anger, frustration, skepticism. Sorrow. In the United States, artists experience acute feelings of marginalization, or they encounter overt hostility. While aware of the cyclical nature of nature and fashion, this remains constant. We are not a nation proud of its choreographers, poets, composers. These are arty *types*, as if a person who fixed your drain was a plumber type, or your broken bones a doctor type. Artists are caricatured, dismissed, easy targets for advertisers; these ads are often covertly or overtly hostile. What would advertising do without art? From what or whom would it get many of its images and ideas? Is there ever a crossover in personnel? Yes. Does this dismiss the distinction between art and advertising? No, regardless of a chorus singing Andy Warhol's name in unison. Some art requires concentration or contemplation; that is suspect. We are a nation of *doers*. Never mind that we do ourselves numb and despairing. Money can be made by some of us feeding others of us lines about youth, beauty, wealth, and what used to be called popularity before its more brittle makeover into fame. Strategies of ambition replace ideas about process, or the frightening pleasure of discovery. If you think this sounds quaint, I am speaking directly to you. Ambition is fine, but it's not an art idea, not a sustaining, long-haul proposition, not if there is nothing to back it up. Cynicism or ennui, besides being a cheap shot, is a mantle, a cloak, a gnawing hotspot of jealousy, envy, and fear, a mark of how terrifying it really is. Art-making, like the life of which it is a part, is messy, unpredictable. Some who want to be part of it, to get close to it but not actually do it, often want the fire but not the heat; they want the perceived glamor but they don't want the struggle; they want the thrill issuing from it, but they want control over it; this is oxymoronic.

We see ourselves as a dynamic people, fed this image by the very medium in front of which we sit, sedentary. Television presents us to ourselves as trim and active, smiling and healthy. Those in media who form the shock troops for corporate product are perhaps testifying to personal experience. Healthy salaries make it possible to maintain the images of health and well-being readily shown. The distance between image and the experience most of us have of ourselves asks that we straddle a huge divide, erodes an already fragile sense of any concept as recherché as truth. Skepticism might have us questioning the entire structure. Cynicism has us shaking our heads as we go out to buy the product. The latter serves its purpose as armor, a complement to the hard-muscled body we are being shown on television. A circle is a perfect shape.

It is difficult for us to sit, active though quiet, responsive though silent. We hold a belief in our right to express ourselves, speak up, be heard. This din, we are told, is participatory democracy *in action*. This is a generous view. Subtlety and patience are not values highly sought by the majority of our culture; it might be that we are so far from them that we are unable to feel their lack, their potential as ballast. Speed and efficiency are stressed, left unquestioned, assumed as positive values; there are unflattering and dangerous precedents for this in our own century. Here we are, sitting down to send or receive e-mail, ask questions of—or respond to—friends or strangers nearby or halfway around the world, change the function to enable us to take a nibble from the enormous data-cookie proffered to us all day, each day, every day and night, track myriad queries-as-quarry through the electronic labyrinth by exerting the slightest pressure on a key or moving an object whose nomenclature will keep lexicographers happy by joining a list of definitions that already include a small rodent, and a dark, swollen bruise under the eye, and we are getting smarter by the minute by being able to access, as it is called, all this info, as we might say, and for a breather, we might go to the gym, swim laps, run on the treadmill, literally, all of which is good for us, *perfectly* good for matching that image mentioned earlier that we will see when we return home, turn on our television set, sit and watch passively before checking our e-mail once more to make sure that we have not missed *anything*. And these are the privileged among us. How do you control large segments of a population that range over a vast landmass, without resorting to overt repression? Create packaged distractions, tangible objects of desire that keep us infantilized, mesmerized as an infant in a crib is by a colorful mobile just out of reach. For an infant, such an object is thought to be a connection to external reality, invigorating, stimulating, leading the eye to privately, quietly contemplate an object in three-dimensional space. Such contemplative time is an unwitting luxury, short-lived. To think of something packaged is to think of something tied up and bound while appearing prettified and neat. By the time we are adults, this pathological externalization, this just-out-of-reachness has translated into a population itchy with unfulfilled, unfulfillable desire; perfect, perfected, hair-trigger mechanisms of repeatedly disappointed wants. Puritan beginnings do not enjoin us from having possessions, only from taking pleasure in them. We have been convinced, continue to convince ourselves, that we do take pleasure in our possessions, but pleasure contains an element of savoring to identify and define it, and there is no time; we are too busy running after the next, and the next. Continue to engage the want, withhold the pleasure. Create debt, then lambast the debtors. Create addicts of all types enslaved to goods, services, dope. Junk. The fix. We are a nation of fixers. For segments of the population that do not obtain privilege but are still saddled with desire, we call in the police.

Connections. The body physical to the body politic, girl-boy, girl-girl, boy-boy, woman-man, woman-woman, man-man: bodies within a cultural milieu, any individual influenced by the society he or she is born into, influencing it in turn, whether actively or by forming part of a statistic which might, in turn, influence the active readers of statistics, some of whom are decision makers. Certain individuals leave marks deeper or longer lasting—on or under the skin—akin to the beauty and pain of a tattoo, disturb the expected surface with a seemingly indelible quality that may take longer to fade, become effaced. Art marks a culture. We are not speaking of privilege. Art is, among other things, a person caught in the act of paying attention. If it were as meaningless as most artists in the United States are made to feel it is, there would not be so much energy devoted to trying to denigrate or co-opt it. Philosophers or the previously mentioned advertisers want to lay claim to it; genteel conservatives and their hysterical cousins on the far right want to destroy it. Art is a magnet. It is a lightning rod, an excuse. All this, while denying that it is anything specific or important. Artists themselves pay lip service to this so as not to appear elitist. This anyone-can-do-it, which becomes a litmus test for whether a person is egalitarian or has the tendencies of a tyrant, is another of the distractions thrown in the path of artists. Anyone has the right to try and create, but it needs to be thought about, passed along, worked at. Writing one poem doesn't make you a poet. Grooving to a tune doesn't make you a choreographer. You cannot implant, clone, or invent imagination. You can be alert, pay attention. If you don't end up making art, you may still become more enlivened, opened up. This does not mean Happy Face.

The six choreographers invited to participate in this project embody the notion of being attentive, alert. Six writings of six makers of movement. Making dances is always writing, drawing: choreo/graphy: each body an appendaged choreographeme, a unit, moving in the act of breath and breathing before all other conscious choices get made or fortunate accidents occur; the awareness of a single, singular breath, freely drawn, wrested from all and every breath belonging to each and all as equalizer, the implicit definition of being born not still, dead, but moving, alive, the internal metronomic clock, tick/tocking, in/out, a primary and passionate intercourse, first and final act. The breath: keeping time as close as the heart, buried not-so-deep inside the ribs, in/out, keeping the last breath at bay by concentrating on the task at hand of hands, feet, shoulders, knees, neck, elbows, head, fingers, wrists, face, oh my my, so many moving parts, and there are more, and the fits thrown by eyes and throats, weeping, shouting, and the air on skin, the bruises, breaks and tears when humans are the material you work with.

What to make of it all? Choreographic decisions, and the dancers that manifest them, are for sturdier hearts than mine. Public consequences in their presence do not deter them. Bows are not anathema, applause not embarrassing. Regardless of the motivation of each, or the intention of a given work, there is generosity in such an act. Choreographers and dancers do not suffer introversion, whereas some writers prefer a dialogue with the dead—an option—while assuming the possibilities of speaking to the not yet born. Even as the ubiquity of an urge for superstardom has become as prevalent as ticks on a deer, writing is open to those of the most solitary and least sociable bent. One to one, that is its primary relationship. Writing gets made alone, then absorbed or glossed in the privacy of living room, bedroom, toilet, or in the private-public space that silent reading occupies on the subway, or in an airport waiting lounge. Words on a page sit still on a flat surface as the eyes move over them; even where words are scrolling on a screen, that screen is flat and the words can be stopped, recaptured, copied. There is not the same sexual connotation given to writers as to dancers—some might say, more's the pity—although they, too, may be romanticized beyond recognition. A person sits down to write, and even though the entire organism is affected—chess masters can lose a noticeable amount of weight though seated during tournament play—it is an image connected for most, if falsely, with only a mental process. Reaction to the word "dancer" is different; we think "body," or "figure." And then, possibly "sex." And then, shame. How culturally-bound is this idea of the body as shameful? Images and words. If we did not have words for procreation, would we still have procreation? Seems likely, observing other species. Dance—in U.S. culture, at any rate—suffers from a perception of body-as-seducer, while we are all being seduced by images that, either covertly or obviously, sell sex. It is confusing, this hypocrisy. There is also the homosexual identification with dancers, especially male. Homophobia is its own punishment, psychically for those whose repression yields it, dangerous and potentially deadly for those on the receiving end of this repression. On the other hand, dance is not given the respect of being viewed historically or politcally in the United States. One of the most telling contrasts in recent memory—and I am not suggesting its like as a sign of being taken seriously—took place in Cambodia, during the inital invasion of the Khmer Rouge at the end of the 1960s and early 1970s; the power of dance was so threatening that dancers were among the first artists killed. Cambodian dances are ancient myths, narratives carried *in* and *by* the body. The Khmer Rouge thought that by killing the dancers, they could help kill the old culture. Dance is the sensual body and the subtle body, the visible and the unseen.

A piece may be worked on for months, for a year or years, then performed rarely and never seen again. Regardless of perceptions to the contrary in regard to sexuality, those who make dances, those who dance them, are most often unwittingly akin to Buddhist monks who spend inordinate time making intricate, multicolored sand paintings, only to sweep them away. The makers and doers of dances accept this exigent reality, accept writing in empty space, accept impermanence, though not without the barrier of hope. They continue their investigations, even as time simultaneously exists and disappears, a slow and constant leak, vapors released from a fumarole.

Some choreographers are also writers but, for most, the silent language of the body is another country with its own vocabulary, and when called upon to use spoken or written language, it is as cue or reminder. Where choreographers do appear in print, it is most often in an interview, or when their work is being written *about*. It is rare that, freed from constraints of topic or theme and with only an approximate word-count to guide them, they are called upon to speak, as writers or users of written words, for themselves. Not all choreographers would wish to. It is a question of change in the medium of exposure; the tension arising from the conflation and dispersion between person and persona that exists in live performance is distinct from the operation of the written. It is an extreme shift in medium, space, time. There is a bewitching hour built into dance. Language-as-making can be intimidating, a strange concept if you have gotten so used to letting go that you don't even question that that's what you are doing by continuing to make dances, and to dance them. Some among the six choreographers in *Footnotes* pursue high physical risk while performing, but feel quite timid about the sustained nature of text, about written language as a means of expressing ideas about their work. Plausible. For others, a single means of expression is not enough to fulfill their requirements as those requirements continue to arise and form, following the initial impulse signaled by the body; they may use spoken language in performance, either memorized or improvised. One of the choreographers in these pages thinks of herself as highly nonverbal in relation to her choreography, but acknowledges using words when working on solos as a key into naming specific movements, as mnemonic device. For others, being able to point to something as tangible as words on paper can be satisfying, can create a sustained dialogue, using written language as another means of expression. The agency of printed, published words carries the potential for a specific inscription in the time-maw. We are still hearing from William Shakespeare, John Donne, Elizabeth Bishop, Zora Neale Hurston, Virginia Woolf, and so many more. Connections.

To become familiar with what the six choreographers in *Footnotes* usually do, you must agree to travel either a long or short distance to where they are doing it. This is asking something. And to really absorb dance—that is, to allow it to enter you and possibly change your life—it is not enough to show up, check it off the cultural consumption list, maintain the well-balanced diet prescribed by the word life*style*.

Do we have to prepare ourselves in a sacred sweat lodge, undergo an arcane ritual, forswear shopping and sweets in order to watch bodies moving through space by some prearranged agreement that signals that this is concert dance? Or to look at a painting? To read or listen to a poem? No. Was it America that hit upon the idea that popular culture should be part of the art discourse? No. Ironically, that was another European import, as we struggle with what it means to be "Made in the U.S.A." It is specious to pretend that pop culture has had to storm the barricades here. Who're we kiddin'? The argument over the rights of popular culture to be seen as valid made sense in Germany in the first half of the century. It strikes an odd chord in the land o' rock 'n' roll, "Make my day," "Show me the money." Hollywood, Las Vegas, the

Disneys, Land and World, all on one continent. There are also other experiences, quieter ones not as readily apparent or immediately accessible as the flicked switch, pushed button. Some ideas take longer to ingest, digest: abstract visual art; free verse; indeterminate sounds or stresses in music. Nonnarrative, nonlinear dances of postmodern choreographers. Disingenuously, many who push popular culture the hardest have a firm grounding in "high" culture. Everything is already in their basket while they shake the pom-poms exlusively for "pop." They host the Carrot-and-Stick, Dog and Pony, American Marketing Show. The same is true where foppish, top-down snobbery prevails. In reality, there is no hierarchy, no contest. There is only paradox, and the proclivity of the person(s) making the work. Art is pleasure, even the sorrowful or painful, not necessarily in the object, sound, or result but in engendering the habit of independent, deep and lasting thought. The *engagement*. Agree to move your own body through space. When you arrive, your role is that of watcher, auditor. It is an utterly important, urgent role. You complete the equation.

It has become increasingly vital that a group of us convene live in a room somewhere, some to perform, others to do the watching or listening. The numbers may not be large. The numbers may equal anywhere from a few to a few hundred. It is agreed that this is not the most efficacious way to sell something to great numbers of people quickly. Dance has nothing to do with dance-as-product. Dance-as-product has nothing to do with the moments, days, months, or years of thoughts rising and falling like breath, the periods of rehearsals needed to transmit an idea from one body to another using eyes, words, touch. Some postmodern choreographers have managers, others wish they did. Others are content not to. All have learned a thing or two about marketing. There is a secret that those who make the work know, and those who market them do not, or pretend they don't: There *is* no dance *product.* There is only this dance or that dance, disappearing as always, reflecting art's concerns with its twentieth century project of redefinition, abstraction, experimentation, an art done by moving figures but far removed, in the modern/postmodern idiom, from the ideals of figuration as it pertains to the historical female form defined by men. Many modern/postmodern dance-makers are female, and have pulled farther and farther away from the vision of dance as hierarchy, both in terms of the stage or space picture and the relationships between and among the participants. This is a reasonable approach to speculations concerning freedom and respect.

Enthusiastic administrators have disseminated information to choreographers on how to write a press release, where to send it. The dissemination of this information is not a negative value, but administrators, or presenters, have not been able to tell the choreographers how to live from the making of dances, or how to get health insurance. Sometimes they go further, and begin to tell the choreographer how to make work, what should or should not be done, what is hot, sexy; which work sells. This is a strategy of control, inappropriate to the interaction between one function and another. Most administrators receive a weekly salary for doing their work. Most artists do not. Art does not need to be saved or managed. It needs to be served, abetted in getting on. Interference and harm differ from form to form. Artists are complicit. Is this suggesting that art be privileged? This is another specious argument in regard to art in the United States. Outrageous levels of resistance are being suggested here to counteract the preposterous idea that art in the U.S. is privileged; not only is it not privileged, it is, in effect, punished. Bite. You must bite. Where one hand reaches out to pet you as you beg, and the other holds the whip, bite. Do it for the ones who have no teeth . . . or spine.

(Another metaphor, a late entry, a sign, in this case, of being exasperated. Vexed. Obsessed. I am among the fortunate, though not among the few.)

Connections to, among, between six choreographers, each having had a certain lasting effect on this specific viewer, a moving image caught as if photographed or seen in a movie, only more, only better, a three-dimensional, unmediated perception in real space/time entering the psyche, a cognizance bypassing analytical function at the moment of seeing, the moment of entry feeling as though stung, shot. Unmediated, not in the psychophilosophical sense of the day but in the sense of seeing something before it is explicated, overdetermined, sold, manipulated as audiovisual overkill, noise and image as a psychic screen obscuring a thing-not-yet-seen. In short, without hype. Hype is essentially a lack of trust. Without it, you can walk into a clear mental and physical space. The art-stricken moment, a moment of dis-ease in the most positive

sense, a shock into further awakening, a dialogue that, once begun, can continue for all the time that is yours.

        Approximately thirty years ago I walked into a small loft and saw
something remarkable, complete; something so mindful it felt as though my skull
had been opened—that's the way I've always described it—and had risen to become
a crown. I saw a woman wearing a sleeveless, jewel-neck, navy-blue dress, dancing
while a man played the saxophone. At some point the dancer lay down on her side,
elbow on the floor, head on her hand, facing us. I think she may have even been wearing navy blue, low-heeled shoes. Whether shod or unshod, she looked quite proper,
conventional. From this position on her side, as the man continued to improvise on
the saxophone—as she was, I believe, improvising her movements—she simply
looked at us while we looked at her. There wasn't much distance between us. What
happened next is something that, three decades later, I am still puzzling over, as if over
a koan. At some inner signal or impulse, the woman rolled toward the audience—no,
the woman was experiencing her body rolling toward the audience. I think that was
it, that she was experiencing, completely, what we saw. She went onto her stomach,
her other side, her back, and came to face us again, only now a bit closer. That's all it
was. It was nothing and it was everything; I saw nothing, and I saw everything. Was.
Saw. Perfect and self-contained, as a palindrome. She did move. It wasn't hallucina-
tory. It was, for want of any better description, the simplest of movements, a distilla-
tion of what it means to go from one particular place or position to the next, similar,
but never the same. It is impossible to experience another's experience, but that's what
it felt like. The woman was the late Judith Dunn, the man, Bill Dixon. She had a grasp
of what continues to keep forming itself in words, after all these years, as "integrity of
movement," its quiddity, the ability to just *be* there with it. I was a young dancer, training to be able to *do.* That moment changed my life, gave me something to contemplate from that time to this, years after I stopped performing as a dancer. When you
see misunderstandings of what she was after—and there have been, and continue to
be, many—it can give new meaning to the words self-consciousness, or boredom.
What I saw was a charged, electrifying moment; it could as easily have been a som-
ersault over a waterfall.

        In this same period I saw a duet by Meredith Monk and Phoebe
Neville. I remember them as having an apparatus over the lower part of their

faces that made a whistling sound as they breathed, looking like two sturdy, clay figures. This is the memory of it; I'm not certain of the veracity. It was in the same loft where I had seen Judith Dunn—Jeff Duncan's, the original Dance Theater Workshop, much documented elsewhere. Within the last decade, I saw the Lucinda Childs Dance Company at the Joyce Theater, work often described as cool, mathematical, but for me, like watching/hearing the music of the rings of Saturn, the dance and dancers leaving me feeling as though fresh oxygen had been pumped through my body. In 1987, I saw the Spanish group La Fura dels Baus in an open-air but gate-locked courtyard in Rotterdam, the Netherlands. It was riveting, claustrophobic, exhilarating, frightening. The spectators were put on the spot, physically under threat, standing, moving, not what we think of as spectators in the usual sense. You needed to be alert to what was being performed in order to not be injured during violent parts of the performance, or hurt by other members of the audience who might panic. I positioned myself near the man who was running La Fura's lights, then moved back into the crowd once I understood where I wanted to place myself in relation to the event. There was nothing passive about the experience. Ironically, the Childs Company performance, inside a theater, felt open, and free; the La Fura performance, outside, engendered awareness of constraints.

Decades ago I participated in a version of *The Mind Is a Muscle*, (Los Angeles, 1969), and so got to work with—to watch—Yvonne Rainer for a couple of days. Ms. Rainer, choreographer/dancer turned filmmaker, remains, visually and textually, one of the most articulate artists working today. *Trio A*, her early dance solo was, like the Dunn performance, a stricken moment for me: fateful, exquisite in that same ability to watch someone privately experience the movement, the moment, while publically performing. Merce Cunningham has always be able to acheive this, even on a proscenium stage.

In May, 1997, I watched Dana Reitz dance at the thirty year anniversary benefit for the Poetry Project at St. Mark's Church. She is attentive to each moment, every gesture, all facial nuance, an indefinable omission of anything extraneous or false, a glyph in space, the dancing/writing body moving in silence. This was embodied dance-text, demanding without any aggression, requiring of you only insofar as you require it of yourself that you see it, hear it, speak with it in its own language, even as you rush quickly to calm yourself down with words, analyze it so that you are not acting like some dumb fan, are bringing reason to bear, ensuring that your eyes, mind, what we used to speak of as heart, do not turn into an analogue of an uruly mob. You know better. You, too, did this for most of your adult life, but still you want to scream and howl because, at such moments—and they are repeated in different forms, here and there—you know why.

(Unabashed, unabated. The foregoing is language as paean, homage, long-due thanks for pleasures contemplated over months, years, or decades, acknowledging impermanence, and the faculty of memory, saying it publicly, in print, for the record.)

Pace, the above, it is the six choreographers in *Footnotes* who immediately came to mind when asked to write this book. All of them have sustained my interest over years of watching their work. I wanted to see them juxtaposed on the page, see what their approaches might be, knowing that each one's relationship to language, as it applies to dance, was quite different. As stated earlier, I did not assign them a specific theme; I am not in the business of assigning tasks to peers; I was more interested to see where they would go without it. We are overwhelmed by handy tips and tasks these days. As each one agreed, it was with the understanding that they would receive space to say whatever they wanted, and a fee. For all the preceding talk of contemporary art and money in these pages, it is true that it has never found an easy relationship in Western culture, though there are always individuals to prove the exception. It is equally true that you cannot readily place a dollar value on a dance or a piece of writing, but until artists can promise their work in lieu of rent, all must be paid: poets, writers, composers, painters, all. Art is not a hobby. First, however, is the freedom of the idea itself, the way of paying attention.

The language pool, the dive into it, inescapable. Even if expressed silently, as thought, we assume its use. It is our errant tool whether spare or profluent, spoken or written. The tongue, hand, and eye are symbiote. The writings that follow cover a range of approaches, from the straightforward, descriptive mode to writing conscious of itself as performance, or aware of its facture. The six distinct voices glance off one another, a game of attention and connections, played by the reader.

part
three

TEXT

IN THE FOLLOWING TEXTS, SOME investigate the medium of written language as invention, while others use it to perform a utilitarian function as illustration of a set of specific tenets or choreographic projects.

All of these choreographers have used, or continue to use spoken language in some or all of their performances, either self-generated, in collaboration with writers, as found material from a variety of sources, or as improvisation.

Written texts of six choreographers, and concomitant responses. They intersect, at points concordant, at others divergent. If we have achieved literacy, we do not have to have this experience overdetermined, mediated, controlled, to be told, as with a step-by-step primer, how to read. We can make our own connections. Art has always been interactive.

Douglas Dunn
Photo: Johan Elbers

i'm dancing

douglas dunn

I'M DANCING I'M INSIDE IT IT'S AS THEY say like giving your own will up to who knows what free from selfish self-made plans so petty so arbitrary aren't they I create what I see on the street I watch out stay inside walk don't walk enough not to get hit plus cue off others for less formal limits shall I jaywalk here do cabs press hard there yes they turn threat-eningly into my crosswalking but this grid to go by only background not the high-tech big-town homecity night-lit multifaceted treasure we eyeballers came for I want sights I organize my personal visual pleasure see facade look sky this girl that guy I make my vision up I choose I look I'm not inside the sights I'm part but apart I trip discover I'm riled someone bumps me I better smile better master guile not leak bile not in New York City it kills style just know well when and where to be tough enough I eat with my eyes myriad surfaces tantalize I don't feel my feet lose the beat turn left take a breath avoid the fight know I'm right I two-step go on feasting.

Daily consciousness is charged with survival and desire, and dancing's is not, is that it?

Warming up to dance thoughts turn I'm still not inside the motion body's on automatic performs dutifully the necessary for physical maintenance and beyond to more stretch greater reach higher jump faster spin to make possible extended unpredictable moves even in stillness no stop plants need water but finish first this twist waist chest prow jump pump land push chase feet headstand wow phone rings cat rubs against leg to continue pause or quit no one's watching no one telling me what to do today but don't let minutes get away the goals known for these hours' ends better follow the plan or whoa slow down what pleasure of course to float on outer currents of ease even an ethos extolling benefits of becalmed mores don't push blood pressure too high too it's cool it's friendly to feel way into minutes' unobvious interstices to follow lead of others' fun I'm susceptible too that subway trip downtown car emptied at Canal I forgot my banal goal got up almost fell to go with them but here instead for sake of inside later time I push the moment down remain outside my stomping ground banish living ladidotty enter student union lobby accept training's levelheaded hierarchy spank slack low-key body elate listless laid back limbs skirt tempting sweet dessert shun seducing ribald fun yank adventurous street-deed weeds simulate synthetic seeds carefully tend this my hothouse torsoed garden aim high at A-prime meta-excellent patient slow controlled growth gradual elaboration correction eventual perfection.

So you use will power now to be better prepared for what you do when later you let go of it. When you're working out are you not dancing?

Moving my beginner's goal to make being in action as familiar as home state back of hand can't miss easy as pie but why if it's then no different from indifferent it still will be this I guarantee if it weren't nobody'd care what other rewards are there though some newer entrepreneurial glad hand jocks crave mainstream esteem squeeze rocks buy money's tree spend ego's fee but what dancer walks De Mille's young cool carefree page thirty-three spree sore feet the rule bent back attack regular painful injury unromantic recovery what if moderns early on had only danced for living wage idea's sage but late we all said we were glad not to be paid because look how far we're laid back confirms our alleged low social studies grade besides why resist who wants to see performers' fists O Terpsichore too much we love to sport the dance you gave us 60's 70's chance enhanced finance to wear pants now again we're white elephants there's more to this pursuit than just getting through it please I beg anyone who has the job to tutor tango bob or weave erase agendas one-two-three cached up many an administrative sleeve pinching Pulcinella's heart domesticating motion's start don't palliate dancing's purgative abnormality continuing climax impossible amoral Tantric antic excitation peak direct ecstasy deep well primordial urge water wading swimming deeply diving wriggling under California's smiling driving houses steps lanes limpid happy seashore weather either.

You want to go to this place called dancing and get to know your way around it as well as you know the landscape you grew up in in California. You maintain that even when this state is completely familiar to you it will continue to be markedly different from, and I get the feeling you mean in some sense better than, the nondancing moment as you know it. And you're anxious that attempts to bring dancing within range of normal societal forces, higher wages, for example, or inclusion as an academic subject, jeopardize the significance of the form for our particular culture by cutting it off from its roots in the nonrational. How'm I doing?

I'm dancing black hole audience pulls inner voice says don't go there what they'll want you won't as if I could indeed anticipate to please magnet without closure's clang OK makes string connecting me to them go twang leaves my picture out of frame but stop even such a simple thought cuts leaves dancer meatless carapace crashing through collapsed space sacrificial sell-short cells up ante play synaptic self-destructive games send static distort picture sorry difficulty please wait some thoughtful steps to correct oh no all flailing falling on not to be disappointed eyes you assume dedicated to premeditated desires save yourself retrench fall in crisis back on what you know breathe deeply ornate arrogant air add virtuosic variations heave clever hype end ego's famine worry not can't get you they this my space I invincibly blind to them I'm safe as clock runs down dance ends I bow they go who cares I fell go eat they'll all forget I too recall through space and time unfolding only me.

I guess you could call that *Variations on Wrong Relation to Audience.* You lose your concentration and the rhythm gets tangled from fear of failure. What would a right relation be?

Dancing reading rehearsed words no breaks momentum plays singing part pry signs apart upend thoughts' stops carry crazed weight on bony chassis link lines unlikely elegant ungainly focus force to nothing's ultimate non-Grand Central cells all equal fight through air's dense fire burns I end ashes leg-brooms sweep earth's cellophanes sway gripeless sequence shapes sea-swell carousel as way to tell business guy it's what you sell unless you fall down hear African chief gives orders lying on back I started dancing to stand up straight you can do that supine too in order to be-long you have to extend then you're involved better know whereof you speak in terms they understand if you don't want to be abandoned provoked response proves you're out there where you want to be but there's out there's sold there's throat too cold to hold forth no meaning binding without cosigning art's lost trust its renegade lust a safe deposit ego trip or ride on Jason's fleeceless ship is that the choice my father's quip bread or inner banner.

Dancing's one thing, marketing another, so? Isn't it more reasonable to make something for which there's already a demand? Or something that uses famil- iar references in the culture so that audience can feel a little at home? Are you convinced that the drive for adulation is too tempting, making the approach unavoidably corrupt? Or are you just bored by conventionality? How do you expect to get people to respond to entertainment if they can't recognize it? And if you don't want to call it entertainment, what's going on, are we sup- posed to be learning something?

I'm dancing a good relation they listen laugh too my funny-tuned bone slides updown hillside *Rille* re-roils mirror reminds finds ring I'm wed to faces seen beyond my own vow do don't ever bow to idle idols repressive passive mythic idylls nor bend at end to them till body's bade farewell to style guile vacant smile reread Adam's pre-dawn gut-guide gently ration lyric reason BLANG BULONG body's million imperative parts erupt up two million screaming smithereens blown to Red Hook Bayside Queens leaf-like flutter down on street scenes almost cease release tight-wound centripetal moral forces force third-eye inner psy- chokinetic focus emergency sinews seek neural solace take tendons' stock re- renew newly diamonds nets umbels spiders glittery wintery nighttime skyline singsong sights image sprites late eighties' *Haole* Jersey's showrooms' fifties' Fords feet falter forget ground ask air it cares it's there to spare if spurn comforting despair's return pare fear test thin skin beg invisible buoys bind body's balance biceps buttocks breast brow seesaw inkling moist eyes twinkling unsure sexy come home bus to nothing.

A bit more optimistic, story-like. You get in trouble but find a way out. What's that at the end, letdown after the show?

Dancing if only meanwhile star tsar victor victim aggressor professor unpersuasive gesture please illumine proper progress muster softer master seduce Medusa hero tyro shaman daimon Islamic team's five reminders grosser goals begone glean green pristine serene joker broker martyr darter seen forget go up go down away unbridle refine display penis present unpresented pleasures eyes behold withheld rebel sibyl dancer bouncer pander pleasure please please lazy eyes' recycled systems' shows for those who go to glow whoa big fellah challenge eye or why not die or win succeed heeding ego's sateless greed sink sinless seed in virgin viewer ruminator communicator receptionist conceptualist deprived inexpressive style suggests something specifies nothing right untrue you can't on stage expunge the page try as might torso's slight verbal vulture culture-master birds' migration goes right past understated underrated doesn't count numbers mount money's fount thinking thanked dance damned thief chief farmer charmer.

I can't tell if you're trying to make sense or to rhyme and make rhythm. It's like watching clouds and they go by before I finish imagining them.

Cavort contra cheap charisma play lucid gruesome fool dance hard at hard to get head down back slumped trust steps lithesome schleps to prove there's more to life than strife I go get lost in deep streams canoe barely afloat ride rapids roiled by scary beasts weird screams then I rest at water's edge dream empty universes' non-beginnings fly back to earth in form of owl soar survey social bowl culture's states current fates everywhere inmates disputations inquisitions this century's proud bowsprit prowess high cognition insufficient small scale killing "clean" blood's willing hand all new natural big-brass-band-brand cruelty canned let's organize bureaucratize incise our eyes bring upscale means myriad teams far finer ways to kill to die am I escaping thus complaining victim's training always raining just as fair full of care making a-political pie doesn't mean I'm getting high on others' woes to change a body's politics get elected vote your shticks dancing's best as jest esthetic sidestep retail gather bail free your feet from Reading Gaol skip turn wobble bend go to Roseland find a friend blend feint turn a phrase bear these death-accepting dances made to break beautifully viewer's willful weather to speed sleepy winter eyes to green.

I see how dancing's important to you, it's where you bring to life feelings you have about what you notice. But finally you don't want to address those feelings, as feelings, explicitly in the work. What is that, escapism? At the end you idealize exchange and change of perception. How would new eyes help?

Dancing's reasons remembered seasons statuesquely posed grotesquely crumbling holiday hindsight Homo's birthright *Walking Back View Unrest Skid Chateauvallonesque* dancing daily mind's melee forms free me settle sadness move remove change address confess

> O Modern Dance, my Eden, my Shangri La
> No persuasion, no promotion, idyll free of greed
> Where prowess dons wit, and we riders
> To the sea follow contour of the land
> Fair nature's sense of form and fun
> Those first to shore who prize her beauty most
> And humble be

horse's sweat crystallized first prize best dressed junior cowboy test despite feet fieldfull still New York City's cacophonous irony appeals unveils ego's grip bruises Caribbean Nutra-Sweet cruise ship trip nervous reaction fear of inaction hide erection avoid detection false direction maybe beeline's better but common truths don't excite eye-saving whitecap foamily bright waves delightfully to break brow frowns drowns bathos brims let's wait and see maybe Modern Maturity will provide clarity increase Qi make lofty an earthly possibility spur me beyond native-born self-discovered Zen-supported no-me identity idolatry.

So you admit you're confused, and sweetly bitter, at least when you take the time to think back. *Unrest* and so on, those are some of your dance titles, right? But your desperate reaction is to careen on, trusting that if you keep to deep rhythms you'll be on the right path. Seems kind of dangerous.

Dancing I have no idea keep going something happens headlines leg-horns arms-deals eye-cons don't fall back on steps you know go stub stutter flow stay inspired quit the past quote the moment moving fast roam unseen shadows'

range avoid deadening habits' pain estranged loves mythic pathways chanted
lines the voice enchimes erase now's later savor trust future's changing flavor

> Last night when I danced
> The world came to me
>
> From every articulation
> Love was flowing
>
> I so radiant
> My expectant audience
>
> Touched by the long reach
> Of my untutored rhythms
>
> Allayed my fears that in this life
> I'd never feel enough

moving bodies miff opinion twisted hips host meaning's minions cancel stop to
disagree dance all night till judgment's free please continue connoisseurs watch-
ers confused anti-elitist curs jaunty fans dancing brokers fellow optimistic
onlookers I beg partake while I'm at all ably still awake shaking coruscatingly
participating witness for bliss not kindness this non-narrative passion roused
worked shot loosed to unforgiving wastes of allegedly expanding un-empty universe feeble fleeting launch-pad kissed tentative thrust carefully crafted catalyst
confirming gist that supposedly we exist.

What a plaint! You truly believe moving will save you, don't you. I must say I'm
touched by your plea that we notice your "existentialist" entertainment. It's as if
meaning is not some culturally contrived add-on, but the fact of your being as
one of us who moves. What would I feel seeing you on stage? I hope you're not
one of those who unknowingly reveals his idea about himself as dancer to be
other than what he is.

Dance dodge display know exactly be able to say what you do disappoint disappear self-delude illusion-prove plight's power mess's merit badlands' bounty

void's virtue interrupt image-making ordain failure as success gloat guiltless as largess flows to those whose shoes fit vulgar feet whose funding fairs vend candied fruit so what if it goes limp for those with inward-turning toes being downcast has it's upside too you know beyond self-congratulation run small roads signed here's salvation just follow sages' cross country recommendation off-track ridge-back rockless esker ask demand reckless focus all-for-nothing dedication endless daily re-education dissipate elation reroute erection eke out reflective penetration seek own backyard seedbed irrigation nurse unknown sometimes ugly flowers feel suspect sometimes evil powers build unique always too tall towers provoke at times friendship's never-wanted glowers follow fame's dream-flame up Jacob's ladder or on your knees as self-proclaimed incinerated canker strive carefree to dive for elemental matter possibly raising eye-tied romantic Terpsichorean praetorians' dander.

Here here, individual voices rising against have a nice day, or riding out wide of celebrity's not OK corral. I've noticed interesting work go underappreciated, dismissed as elitist, or whatever, yes. Yes, the rules governing what becomes exemplary are often non-aesthetic, even in times when formalism's in favor. And yes, one is led willly-nilly to wonder how much our historical culture heroes come to us through influence peddling. But these matters aren't solvable, so why go on about them?

Dance ironic confidence pretending to be someone you're not be the one pretending to be the someone you're not be the one pretending to be the someone pretending to be the someone you're not and on and on to have a dance that matters most but doesn't boast it's killed the ghost how could anyone else or I present the body as if it's chaste a childhood why without at least a cloud unknowing to calm claim we see sky's eye or are they ready today not I to say it's really me you see that here's enough this earthly stuff such bluff deserves rebuff doesn't content my feet's desire to dance on green-grass firmament I'll not relent and if indeed you pretend to show high-end I insist you send up upend your dancing friend rend smooth surface of false purchase poke devil's tail twixt lustrous legs strike poses extra-literally match music ultra-faithfully fall freely away from ought-to-be know what makes no-meaning easy to see it's letting go of what you keep in tow assume layered reality's availability to all who float on clouds winds waft beyond world's past and future's predictably brash originality.

A proto-manifesto? Let's see, you believe that feeling can fly directly off the dancer's body into the spectator's and become thought, or basis of thought, or new intuition. You hope you're giving something, but are clear verbally only about what it isn't. Perhaps to challenge audience into new consciousness. Maybe you need audience that's smarter than you. Or maybe you want them to think they are.

Dancing effortless receiving here come comets streaming 3-D etchings imports sylvan silk-screens dreaming stretch move flesh gleams lightening longer limbs muscles' magic fast-through-back un-flat trajectories smack vivacious velocities veer vectorlessly hums skim skin's shimmer north-south laser's sideways signals send Arctic Caribbean blue-green seas palm-tree bullmoose reveries tease moist thighs widen knock knees' wobbling gyres ignite groin's Faustian fires loosen high-leg hip-joints' needs to please allow pelvis's fundamental undulatory ease reroute reason merge myriad fourfold seasons suck sense-around stamens' tension mix beehive's queen-led drone-driven sting-bled catacomb socialist cohesion emanate tongue-flicked slingshotted honeyed gentian reach treetop's highest flower trace ship-chain's deepest anchor battle black jack's right-left power conjurer kowtows facing vibratory joker's trump-card force-field's consummate fleet-foot bower.

I get the pattern, you start out dancing, so to speak, get sidetracked by an overactive, sometimes moralizing word-brain. In this one you don't stray as much. I see what you mean by layered, the punning on "bower" at the end is so submerged as to be invisible. But the sounds, and the listener's mind at work to collect the assertions and the passions pushing up through make for a consistent bouquet, as in a room full of arrangements, the stanzas made up of varied configurations of the same flowers.

Dance unaimed affect ironic irony's *Rubble Dance* bubble ape scorpion's self-stabbing thorn-horn go for broke unchoked charged new year's anti-resolution resolution no holds held sole help inner others rigorously shaped unfamiliar beauty duty to outer whither weather winning booty moot staged performance simulation unemotionless actual instantaneous recapitulation embody vatic strategy don't fall back on anything unseen opening accidentally something aesthetically obscene the mouth of N for example doesn't scream don't admonish me to be mean don't cast specious spell saying anything stainless sells bell ball bull bowl bric-a-brac the Book of Kells to reconfigure arrow's tip target pocket ferret friends maintain docket punish disruptive insubordination spurn counterfeiters' advantageous situation continue instead enhancing eye-hand coordination aspersions due to persons who guarding their goods dis Robin Hood what life-bound animal even however would settle for less than fully entitled mettle praise and grazing pastures green with all withal beholding every scene.

Maybe I'm wrong to try to extract clear meanings in terms of thoughts I already have. When I try less hard to grip ideas I end up feeling giddy, or sad. In any case it's not hard to see that your confusion about art and commerce is a fire out of control in a forest too green to die.

Rockets' red glare ego's still there stealing current rages' pizzazz ungyved smiley high-five jive hustler's snake oil razzmatazz usurps underdog's genuine pre image-is-all appeal abuses explanation expectation public's unctuous TV-sized trust vicarious despair half-realized lust or bust truth be trussed fancy narcissistic prancing tactical sentimental dancing how 80's commercial worthy how Venice come-get-me curvy haughty artistic atrophy warrants hardy aesthetic antipathetic commentary not toupee trophy necklace winner wards off searching sold-out doubt routs need to void veneer don't say fame's fearsome everyone knows false sincerity sells assures all's well adulation's warm glow stimulates career flow fosters faster to and fro invites fake makes unnecessary risky true manifesto brings voice in range of any age in guise of innovation sustains convention gives easy reading chance to turn page in short extends good life of what you have to say tempting you as adversary to unpremeditated play to splay yourself on wheel of fortune join marching force unison motion make invention a pat fact hyped sensation one more voraciously media-ized exploitable emotion.

That was rather harsh. Are you talking to an inner or an outer figure?

Dancing success nemesis cross to bear failure's allure also albatross to wear one the two fair body true or trick flair hairdo frankly crafted gift artifice or blackhearted bait sharp-honed gaff neither ought be task-central both become mega-mental who says so I do I judgmental oh good grief he's gone compartmental lost that naive all-accepting mantle OK hit it wake penitential think exponential act experiential choose fit muse light lifelong fuse pay mammon's dues identify blues' hues deliver personally observed objectified news leave tantalizing readable clues for crews who to visit movement's ken cross space-time's now-where-when see you spin ride rhyme mastering zero-gravity mime disabusing mind's right to climb inventing to stop an indeterminate dime it's no crime to follow line of least resistance disable persistence coddle concupiscence unless of course you care to see rock-crease weed evil deed steady steed silent reed.

You try to avoid judgments, but once you let a few out you seem freed to state more clearly your own ideals and direction.

Trying is trying trying not to is trying only not trying is not trying bragging is bragging not bragging not bragging trying not to brag about not bragging arrogant modesty hides what's to see well-held skillful neutral me viewers' lulled pleasant lands' formalities no demands no taking stands not true really could be ideal intentionality to fly beyond personality toward anarchistic polity sensitive tolerant self-control no jealousy heightened loving sensual aesthetic stimulation awestruck earthly in-out out-in meditation constant dizzying appreciative consternation sky's radiant tempting explanation dancing's anyway inconvenient means of inner life display suggests states relies on actions' shapely fray dancer's will at bay alerts eye's mind to today acknowledges lifetime's decay registers ongoing replay incites lost body's best hooray saying it is and it's not OK.

I'm getting better at rolling with the density, that one took me right with it. I'd say you like your assertions still in touch with the impulses they start from, but consider them inadequate, incomplete until paired with their opposites.

Which then dancing non-mimetic is it redirected self-threatening throb hand one hand two inspired vision Platonic homiletic how assert non-assertive policy how agree to disagree still be me see my foes clearly cut leash get life's lease continue to increase no expense to others' rents get past stupid nervous stunts go as far as smart heart wants hitting hard shunning bunts catching passes running punts for touchdowns home town hoe-down art-found rebound manifest toe expressionistic stasis formalistic flow contradictory continuity maximally fluctuating homeostatic basis rhythmically responsive ruminative crasis tacit fear-entangled uncontrollable passion determined sacrificial simply periphrastic anti-fashion clear confusion resolutely imposed non-resolution easy as that excise fat hero goes splat pet the cat work hard watch wait for death's bureaucrats to issue next ineloquent fiat.

So the particular feelings underlying your work put you in conflict right away about how it does or does not get seen. You might say that its implicit subject is performance as metaphor for presentation of self, and that that self is ever struggling to find a fully justified way to be present. But what's the point of that presence without others as at least witness? Doubt, indecision, arbitrary hopeful inconclusive assertion. Around and around. You don't want to make ambivalence as content explicit and intentionally involving because to do so would be to be in fact decisive, would drop the work into the familiar psychological mill of conventional story-oriented theater and idea. Something like that?

My dancing making fun is my dancing making fun of my dancing's making fun of my dancing's making fun of my and others' dancing why not serious calm straight could be afraid closed-gate staid could be clown's antic question exalted tall gods' gifts are we or salted Homo fricassee evolution's final premier selection or devilish universe's dyspeptic digestion hubristic dormer adorns former latter risks razing roof line altogether what would it be dreaming to see Bali Rhapsody inspired parody harmonious cacophony asparagus grows out my head fingers mimosa tendrils wind-wriggling lichen-o'ertaken thighs green internecine ivy battles gray spots hopped right foot rooted arched throat calls across canyon palm fronds' cracks answer sunsets' ultraviolets invite waterman airfish skyheather earthstar.

Are you trying to be difficult, different? Do you have—somewhere I read you should—a good reason to tax linguistic convention? What if there is a reason, that I don't get, and you know it? Oh dear oh dear. I'd say your form implies an ambivalence about talking, at least talking about dancing. Movement has its conventions, and you trust your intuitions in that language. With words you find a denser, more linear network of logic and association that you know to be familiar to most people as the standard lens through which to view the world. Using words-about to establish the primacy or essential difference of something immediate, wordless, sensorial, is that what you're worried about? You don't want your dancing thoughts turned into fixed-by-word ideas, reified into static concepts, arrogated to self-assured academic parlance? Why, because the latter stimulate only our phoneme-loving cells and act as a soporific on the rest? What are you, a disgruntled child of the Enlightenment? I'll admit, our word-first posture has ended up giving us a false sense of control. We avoid. Something's missing. We can't decide whether we need more command over or better integration of disparate aspects of our natures. Whenever our conspiratorial suppressive consensus is broken there's always someone there to shore it up: He was such a nice boy, I can't believe he would do such a thing.

One more guileless strident sally as if the perfect smile of ballet weren't enough to counter gruff now these new-breed modish moderns with their lenient feel-good gol-darns siphon guilt-foundations' coffers offer golfers trapless fairways even greens cups as big as restaurant tureens passive art's pallid par all-inclusive unabusive I'm so glad that from now on we're all for community folk-like dancing no more alienated highfalutin' intellectually elitist effete prancing exit anger discontent camp's Lone Ranger aesthetic danger kill the snobs purge their jobs respect the mob's thingamabob opinions pluck unmarketable pinions let's all be equally dumb it's so much more fun knowing sequel follows prequel whoopee a sarcasm spasm please forgive me the function of art is to start the heart beating without compunction without scorn or unction after making it miss several pulses as it falls crawls jumps convulses a russet unicorn barely crossing an unfathomable abyss breathed as aesthetic artifice deeper than any heretofore risked.

You're making a connection between more accessible performance and the right-wing attack on artists? Hmm. I guess you're feeling the pressure of both specific and undifferentiated indifference or disdain. In any case I like it that you backed yourself into a corner and felt obliged to come up with a definition, when to do so goes against the grain of what I infer you would like: unopinionated dancing.

There's a new kind of body dancing in Manhattan these days and it's interesting to watch only for a few minutes, especially on proscenium stage. Instead of stretching, it hangs; instead of extending, it throws; instead of descending, it lets go. As it depends to begin on momentum of launched weight, it must each time recover, so its frequent denouements are predictable. Unable or unwilling to jump, to show a sustained position in air, it offers neither the realization nor the promise of activity in the upper third of the available vertical axis. Uninterested in turnout and the possibilities this trained rotation of the leg affords for moving through space with fast changes of direction, the body is content with limited horizontal exploration as well. The flabby connectivity of torso and limbs and the redundant restarting of the necessarily short phrases invite a collapsing of the surrounding space. The result, no matter how unimagistic the movement, is the same as with psychologically and emotionally focused forms that eschew shape as a primary concern. Watching, you sense that something is aimed at heart or brain, without your eye being part of the target. Harder and harder you look, with a narrower and narrower lens. Soon the landscape, the context which makes the dancer real, be it the stage itself in dancing as such, or the fantasy world of a more illusionary form, is gone. You're left with a split-off figure, dancer not as substance but as idea. This body seems to desire to appear less stylized, more casual, more pedestrian than other theater bodies. But in denying a proportion the theater eye comprehends, it speaks only as concept, sacrificing the opportunity to provide the viewer with more than a thimbleful of psychokinetic experience, nonassociative or otherwise. Oddly, this seeming-on-the-one-hand-to-want-to-be-average body, in fact on the other emanates a vigorous narcissism, the motive of which is puzzling. Does the exaggerated show of irrelevant satisfaction derive from this body's feeling it's healthier than another? Less enthusiastic? Better at hiding enthusiasm? More democratic? More abstract? Less communicative? Less arrogant?

So you CAN speak clearly, or should I say conventionally. I know what you mean about the spectrum of muscle and mentation. Some present athleticism as enough, others an idea about the body and its behavior in which the dancer appears as bloodless symbol. Oddly, as you suggest, the latter appear to want to be considered more real, in a life versus art sense, as if anything on stage could avoid automatically being style. It was eye-opening when the demand to see walking as dancing was first made. Cooler was hotter when hotter was boiling over. Without a counter for cool, either a too hot outer or a pressurized inner, or both, cool's but cold. Pedestrianism, movement understated in its visual aspect, as a primary approach hasn't much to offer the once-opened eye. At least not yet. I've wondered if the style might be interesting taken in the direction of acting.

Versus work pretended heaven sent is a tried-to-dance look too hard to see whoa my thirty-year legacy unremitting spree indicting others' struts undermining any own upward princely juts coming on striving awkward light-o-teasingly disguising hidden angles weaving something tricky viewers to untangle not abuse elated generous ruse change shoes leave clues unsign style shun obvious smile assume public's extra mile smart-eyed bulls see enough shows fearlessly to grope grasp opus's self-oppositional cast deadpan's task-mask alas work's meta aspect undetected paranoid sad frets no regrets avoid explanation it subverts appreciator's experiential exploration risky choosing committed feeling honest dealing makes for overexcited personality glorification encourages audience exploitation while conversely aesthetic obstacles open up obvious observations to obloquy no more oh-boy joy they jump like okapi athletic facility silly absent mean mill grinding gross findings to kinetic Eros.

It's good to hear you trying to say what it is as well as what it's not. But with the amount of intimidation many people feel about art in general, your work, part of the meaning of which is its lack of various kinds of obvious appeal, requiring of them a leap to approach it, is bound to play right into the hands of those who are now successfully, at least where sword is money, killing off what they call elitism. I hear your implicit question, what kind of art do those who don't want high art want? Or, does equal access demand the dismemberment of excellence? But you don't appear ready to do more than state an objection on a subject that could produce helpful ideas if elaborated.

Wanting to take you with me on every dance's itinerary showing concretely each shaped display each considered kinetic essay each vertiginous stay each next time-borne continuity leaving you by avoiding pedagogy story psychology simultaneously free to indulge whatever fantasy keeps your focused attention company submerging idea eye offered primarily cloud-flecked open-sea skyscape froth-clad Nereidian Neptunian wave-plashed unreined newfound beauty orgy come-melt-me non-defensive not offensive either panoply bodily carefree array rigorous fancy witty paradisiacal parade dancer's live presence shades delicately invades artifact's might fades ephemeral intimations give dance low-grade stance in art-historical parlance plus best chance to evince and enhance value of momentary glance self-discovered balance head-heart-leg correspondence physically interpersonal interdependence spatio-temporal free-

lance independence not to mention various endorphin-driven not to be shriv-
en vicariously available sometimes salable extravagantly ecstatic eternally mem-
orable incredible enchantments.

Leaving out many of the little words is like leaving out moldings and trim in
architecture. You see the different materials butting startlingly up against one
another and your eye works to join them to unify the structure, or not.

Need for others' empathic consideration own self-identification shrink territory
open to exploration don't blink you're still in the pink send doubt on vacation
intern isolation organize elation slay frustration nourish ignition jettison tradition except to mitigate repetition ignore inanition don't castrate cognition enjoy
palpitation dance submerged circus relatively smooth surface cliff-edge's performance ridiculousness mend material money matters personal emotional nondance tatters escape word's temptation remove studio's study station honor
decision eschewing charm schmoozing backbiting harm i.e. all extracurricular
persuasion trust audience even culture-hero sycophants presenters power brokers of the dance to understand ambivalence insecurity unsurity as serious kind
of clarity complex variety sort of simplicity stay down front do what you want be
bountiful fount flowing out over beautiful million-eyed tapestry.

You seem to be coming sufficiently to terms with your fear-filled defensive arro-
gance to want to continue to put work out into what you feel is an imperfect,
corrupting environment. You even begin to describe and define your dancing in
ways that might help others to see into it. It seems you began to dance as an
escape, but a form of escape that also kept you connected with at least a distanced sense of who others are. Hearing you I feel you're getting ready to see
them more clearly, friends or foes, and not only to continue to work, but also to
acknowledge without backing down their responses to it. Am I right?

—1997

commentary

IMAGE

A man driving an open vehicle drops roadblocks along a route, goes away, circles, drives along the route again, confronts the roadblocks: "Well, I'll be. Roadblocks." Genuine surprise. The man is not inattentive, forgetful, unintelligent, naive. He is inside the moment, now is now is now is now is now. Confronting the roadblocks, he spontaneously, but with care, removes them one by one, puts them in the open vehicle again, repositions them, drives on, places the roadblocks along another stretch. Goes away, circles. Comes back, confronts. "Well. I'll be. Roadblocks. D'you see that? What d'you think?" Each time new, and not a horizontal Sisyphus. This man is not condemned owing to greed. This man is *not* condemned at all, and if he is, it is to love.

REFLECTION

Douglas Dunn's "I'm Dancing" begins stripped of punctuation. The effect is not unlike seeing a naked person in the middle of the street: it grabs our attention.

Part of Dunn's overall text is structured as an a-stanzaic prose-poem-as-essay, one which attempts an end run around ego and intellect-as-blockade. This aspect presents a labyrinthine "inner" voice, Dunn as artist, specifically as dancer/dance maker/performer. The other, "outside," voice sets a self-reflexive dialogue in motion, posits a wry and savvy, though not unkind, interlocutor, willing to learn more, dressed in conventional commas and periods. (When the dancer-voice makes a foray into conventional punctuation toward the end of "I'm Dancing," it is to analyze a current movement style Dunn finds questionable in contrast to its founding impulse, in which Dunn played some part).

Undergirding "I'm Dancing"—whose title makes clear where, among other possible interpretations, Dunn's loyalties lie—is one implicit declaration, one implicit question, and a concern about the *Footnotes* project itself; there is also an awareness, throughout, of the relationship of dance-making to economics. The declaration begs the very question of the split: "You might say that [Dunn's dances'] implicit subject is performance as metaphor for presentation of self, and that the self is ever struggling to find a fully justified way to be present" (p. 56). It enunciates the art-self/other-self fine-line-that-cannot-be-but-crossed when an artist sets out to explicate, in words, a self apart. The act of writing about it obviates the duality. You cannot write as an artist about the artist writing about the self not being the artist. In dance, the body inhabits and exhibits a different, but not entirely unrelated, paradox: We are seeing an idea, not a body, though it is a body, not an idea.

Contained within this labyrinth of art-self/other-self as it relates specifically to Dunn's decades-long choreographic project is the question he poses, which might be said to be the thorn in the faun's hoof: "[W]hat kind of art do those who don't want high art want?" (p. 59). Dunn does not strike me as a man who would ban rock 'n' roll. Yet here is a crux. It highlights the distinctions between or among naming, characterizing, and labeling. Douglas Dunn (naming) is a white, male, heterosexual of a certain chronological age whose work is marked, in part, by arcane references, some of which are to centuries-old European art (characterizing). This makes Dunn elitist (labeling). Not. Elitism carries a suggestion of permission, restriction, a "May I?... You may," form of address, a granting. This does not occupy any place in this artist's discourse. Anyone is invited to the party, can attend. What can we say of that which we may not already know? That it can constitute a riddle, a puzzle, a mystery; it can arouse our curiosity, titillate, teach without being didactic. It can be viewed as a game, one with a built-in opening move in the form of all the information in front of our eyes. We can read Dunn's gambit in his writing. Does the work exemplify mass appeal? I would say not. Doesn't that make it elitist? No. Requiring that all art have mass appeal before it is not labeled elitist creates a potential for cultural leveling, which is a dangerous, and suspect, agenda. There is a vast territory, over which most artists range, between these aribitrary definitions of what consititutes art for the few and art for the many. It is possible to listen to, distinguish among, prefer, or appreciate the differences between, for example, James Brown *or* Balinese gamelan, salsa, hip hop *and* Bach, to honor and make use of them as the artist sees fit. There is no contest set up by the music itself, no problem with the structure of the ear.

References abound in any art form; Dunn's choreographic work is rich in them. In "I'm Dancing" there are echoic traces of and borrowings from popular culture, *Hoch Kultur*, and what might be termed mid-range cultural artifact, that which was popular in its own time, but has been recontextualized in ours. In Dunn's text we can read the sounds or rhythms of rap, Shakespeare, James Joyce, English seventeenth century poets on their way to a meeting with the nineteenth century's Gilbert and Sullivan, even faint murmurings of Dr. Seuss and Lewis Carroll, though this list is not exhaustive. Still, it is all Dunn's impulse that drives and shapes the text, laying claim to dances he has made through naming them, costumed as a puckish ventriloquist throwing—and thrown by—the voice, wondering how and how much to reveal.

It has been written of Dunn, and those with whom he collaborated early on, "[D]ancer-choreographers [in Grand Union][1] were as articulate with words as they were with movement. . . and engaged in all sorts of word wit."[2] These experiments continued to break the sound barrier, assayed the concept of the dancer as dumb—whether stupid or mute—and further elaborated the discussion in regard to structure/content/self. This long-ago experience did not, in the present, stop Dunn from questioning, "Using words to establish the. . . essential difference of [dance, which is] something immediate, wordless, sensorial . . . [not wanting]. . . dancing thoughts turned into fixed-by-word ideas, reified into static concepts . . ." (pp. 56—57) Despite these doubts, Dunn is able to talk about dance while considering writing as praxis on its own terms.

Through the medium of written language, Dunn addresses the conflicts and questions on view, however encoded, in "I'm Dancing": the tensions existing among subject, the "it" of the thing we endeavor to do, and the external milieu, including the economic, with its practical and symbolic value, the "Why would anyone continue to do this, when it is so hard?" He eloquently frames this fracas in relation to its goad when he writes: "*[C]onfusion about art and commerce is a fire out of control in a forest too green to die.*" (p. 54, italics mine).

AFTERIMAGE

A lithe man of serious demeanor chassés, skips, *cavorts* around a space, arms seemingly akimbo, eyes changing focus as though, in the midst of all that his body is doing, he is searching for some important, missing object though he dare not stop moving long enough to find it, and we are not really supposed to know he is looking.

notes

1   From 1970 to 1976, choreographer-dancers Becky Arnold, Trisha Brown, Barbara Dilly [Lloyd], Douglas Dunn, David Gordon, Nancy Lewis, Steve Paxton, Yvonne Rainer, and Lincoln Scott worked together under the name Grand Union, an outgrowth, in terms of most of its personnel—though Dunn was not included in their number—of the Judson [Church] group of the 1960s (see below).

2   Sally Banes, "Dancing on the Edge." In *Writing Dancing in the Age of Postmodernism*, (Hanover, NH: Wesleyan University Press/University Press of New England: 1994), 256—257.

Marjorie Gamso
Photo: Laine Whitcomb

cover(t) stories

marjorie gamso

I AM SEARCHING—SEARCHING THROUGH my handbag, through my desk, my bookshelf, my dictionary, my childhood memories — searching everywhere for words to describe the way movement phrases that I bring to rehearsal begin to change as soon as the rehearsal starts, how after several rehearsals the phrases have begotten phrases that bear only the slightest resemblance to them. I am searching for words to describe the feverish and futile, hilarious and hysterical efforts that the choreographer/director and dancer/interpreter, even when they are the same (divided) person, go through to retrieve the now forgotten phrase, but ...

•   •   •

FOR THE MOMENT, I am thinking about *Hamlet*, a tale, I think you know it, of royal decadence and deceit with a hint of the supernatural that could well be the cover story for a weekly gossip magazine. I am thinking about Hamlet, the central character in the story, who, with his insider's view of corruption in high places, had he written down his observations, could easily have sold them to some scandal sheet of the day for a good price—if his vocation were for journalism. It wasn't. The Prince of Denmark would not, of course, have been expected to have a "vocation."

But unexpected things—or only half-expected things—kept happening to Prince Hamlet, and . . .

FOR THE MOMENT, I am thinking about *Hecuba*,[1] a tale, I wonder if you know it, of a woman who ceased to care how she died—or rather, of how a woman ceased to care who she was when she died, or rather, of how death stalked a woman who believed herself to be already dead. It's a complicated tale. Let me try to recall for you the background against which it is told: a savage, nine-year war has ended; at first a minor international dispute, a quarrel over an adulterous affair between Paris, a Trojan, and Helen, a Greek, the wounded honor of Helen's abandoned husband Menelaus serving the Greeks as a fine cover story for a military move against the wealthy Trojan state; when Troy, predictably, resisted, full-fledged war ensued, and at the instigation of high-born men and well-placed gods (for, it must be added, Paris and Menelaus both were high-born men upon whom high-placed gods bestowed their favors), virtually every city-state in the region became caught up in this war that was later to become known as the "Trojan War." For it was on Trojan soil that the final battles were fought. And it was Trojan soil that was scorched and blood-reddened, and in the end it was the Trojan people who were defeated. Hecuba had been their queen. It is Hecuba's tale that I am thinking about.

I am thinking of the moment when, still uncertain how he is to interpret events as they are unfolding around him, Hamlet meets a troupe of actors who have fallen into disfavor in their native country and come to entertain the Danish Court.[1] It seems that they have met before, the prince and the players.

Hamlet remembers being in a different time, a different place, and hearing one of them recite Aeneas' tale to Dido. He asks if he might hear the speech again. The actor obliges. He begins to speak of the atrocities of war as if he were Aeneas recollecting what he witnessed as a soldier—the clatter of swords, the flow of blood, the spread of fire, the suffering of those who fell in battle and of those who watched the falling and survived to mourn the fallen—as if he, like Aeneas, heard the cry of mortal suffering that came from vanquished Troy's Queen Hecuba, who, having seen her loved ones slain before her eyes, was howling at the flames, the winds, the war, just howling into space. Hamlet, hearing the actor recall (in performance) what Virgil recalled (in writing) what Aeneas recalled (in memory) what Hecuba called out (in

Already old when the war began, the war had made her very old—old enough to have grandchildren as well as children and a husband to mourn, old enough to have become mourning itself, to have become pure mourning—yet she had survived it. And now she, like every Trojan who survived, was interred in Thrace, awaiting the transport vessel that would carry her to Greece where she would dwell in servitude, a slave of the people who had conquered her people—if she was still alive after the slave ship voyage. Can Hecuba have expected to survive such a journey?

"Shorn of greatness, pride, and everything but life" (l. 57), she faced the (im)possibility of survival without expectations. Yet the unexpected came to her—first in a dream, then exactly as dreamed. As dreamed, of her remaining children, one, a daughter, Polyxena, whose beauty had attracted Achilles when he arrived in Troy where he was soon to die (triumphantly) in combat, now was summoned by the great war hero's ghost, a sacrificial offering, "the blood of the living to sweeten a dead man's grave" (l. 41), while another, a son, her youngest, one far pain), understands what he hears as a call to theater. Not yet a "vocation," perhaps, but Hamlet is in possession of an "idea for a piece." He acts quickly now, contracting with the actors to participate in the development of his "idea," setting a date for the performance, etc. I've been through this routine, and I am now thinking . . .

No, I will let you in on what Hamlet is thinking:

> Is it not monstrous that this player here,
> But in a fiction, in a dream of passion,
> Could force his soul so to his own conceit
> That from her working all his visage wanned,
> Tears in his eyes, distraction in his aspect,
> A broken voice, and his whole function suiting
> With forms to his conceit? And all for nothing,
> For Hecuba!
> What's Hecuba to him, or he to Hecuba,

too young to have engaged in any war maneuvers and entrusted to Polymestor, a supposed family friend in a supposedly neutral land to wait for war's end, was found to have been murdered, his body thrown to sea by that very false friend who, when he learned of Troy's defeat, saw in it an opportunity to profit. Hecuba endured the loss of her children twice—first through dreaming eyes, and then a second time through eyes awake with terror. To those who offered her pity, she replied that she was beyond it, already dead: "I died long ago. Nothing can touch me now" (l. 783).[2]

Now, Hecuba, who recently had been a queen and knew the rules that monarchs were obliged to follow, knew that Polymestor had committed an assassin's act, loathsome to the gods and punishable under international law. She wondered if she might persuade the Greeks who now ruled over Troy to invoke that law and punish the murderer of her son. She (who was without expectations) appealed to King Agamemnon with this legal argument; he turned away. Then she (still the unexpectant one) made her appeal more personal, reminding him that since among the Trojan goods he'd plundered was her last remaining child, her daughter Cassandra, he might have an emo-

That he should weep for her?
What would he do

Had he the motive and the cue
for passion

That I have? He would drown
the stage with tears

And cleave the general ear with
horrid speech,

Make mad the guilty and appall
the free,

Confound the ignorant, and
amaze indeed

The very faculty of eyes and ears.
(II, ii, 578–93).

You will have noticed that he does his
thinking in the conditional mode, the
mode of wishful thinking, of desire that
already imagines the consequences of its
fulfillment and taunts the desirer with
the terrifying image of his dream come
true. It is the mode of hallucination: the
hallucinated performance has ended;
the hallucinated stage is drenched with
tears; the hallucinated spectators are
stunned; those who are guilty, those who
are free, those who are ignorant, each has
been shattered by the truth of what s/he's
seen and heard. Theater or theater's
"Double?"[2] If theater exists, as Hamlet
will later theorize when speaking to his
cast for the last time before leaving

tional stake in handling a case involving his concubine's younger brother;
again he turned from her. She called
him back. "Be like a painter," she
cried, "Stand back, see me in perspec-
tive, see me whole, observe my
wretchedness" (l. 808), turning the
appeal into spectacle, performance.
And when he turned away again, she
knew, as she had always known, no
words she could combine could ever
make him (the conqueror) take up
her (the conquered's) cause, but still
she could not stop herself from
speaking. For "One more word," her
tongue called out from deep inside
the dungeon of her mouth. And there
escaped a torrent:

If by some magic, some gift of
the gods,

I could become all speech—
tongues in my arms,

hands that talked, voices speaking, crying from my hair and feet—
then, all together

as one voice, I would fall and
touch your knees, crying, begging,
imploring   with   a   thousand
tongues —

O master, greatest light of
Hellas,

hear me . . . (l. 835)

You will have noticed that she
speaks this passionate speech, this

them on their own with their own ways of preparing for performance—"To hold the mirror up to nature" (III, ii, 19), then its very existence denaturalizes, for the mirror reflection is virtual nature, nature's double. Was the call of the theater that reached Hamlet's ears while he listened to the actor's recitation a "true" calling or a phantom call?

Knowing the tale, and I think you do, you will now remember that before his fateful meeting with the troupe of players, Prince Hamlet had received another phantom call.[3]

"Remember me" (I, v, 91), the phantom caller had insisted before departing—for who knows where, exactly? And surely Hamlet would remember every word the phantom spoke. The line would have been easy for him to memorize, already half-expected when he heard them. As to the identity of this phantom visitor who had come to him "in such a questionable shape" (I, iv, 43), however— can a phantom's contours ever be identified (with) with certainty?—he had persistent doubts. How could he, then, be certain he was right for the role he was being called upon to play in the phantom's drama, which it seemed,

speech about speech—or rather, about the impossibility of speech, or rather, about unheard of possibilities for speech; a complicated speech it is—in the conditional mode, the mode of wishful thinking, of desire that already imagines the consequences of its fulfillment and taunts the desirer with the terrifying image of her dream come true. The body that Hecuba hallucinates, a body of tongues, of chattering hands and screeching hair is truly monstrous— monstrous to behold, but also unbearable to be. With tongues proliferating everywhere, each one having its own native dialect and all of them always getting in each other's way, it is a body over which one can exert no control. It can communicate nothing but its desperate need to communicate, which, of course, is not exactly nothing.[3]

("Is it not monstrous," then, to imagine—as I do when I begin to make a dance—that my body can somehow take over at the point where "words fail me?" Yet this point of desperation is in fact the point of departure. Later, when rehearsing, through the interaction that takes place between choreographer/director and dancer/interpreter, was certain to become his drama? It is at this point that Hamlet, the central character in the tale called *Hamlet,* is first struck by the monstrous nature of performance—"That one may smile and smile and be a villain" (I, v, 8)—and it is at this point, too, that he decides to go forth and mingle with monsters, to become one himself, to adopt a mask, an "antic disposition," to practice a kind of performance art.

Hamlet has perhaps been "doing" performance already when he formulates his "idea" for a performance piece. Once he's done so, despite his reputation for self-centered and aristocratic idling (both at court and in the many commentaries on his character that have been written and continue to be written), he works quickly. He is possessed of an "idea;" he needs to be dispossessed of it, not to take it through an arduous rehearsal process at the end of which it may be transformed beyond recognition.

(This was the routine as I understood it when I made my first dances. Like Hamlet speaking to the players, I thought that if performers neither underplayed nor overacted, the "idea" that I possessed—or that possessed

even if I am occupying both positions, something else can happen, the unexpected, or the half-expected. And this is why I find myself thinking about Hecuba at the moment when she doubts her cover story as I attempt to understand my own covert story and the cover stories I have sometimes made up when asked to describe my work. But I must return you now to the Thracian coast where Greeks and Trojans bide their time, for no ship can leave the harbor until the wind turns in its favor.)

Winds determine many fates. This is Hecuba's. With no hope of justice from a higher power, she recalls another power that her sex (Hecuba, an old woman without expectations, remembers her sex) knows how to use.

> Women killed
> Aegyptus' sons.
> Women emptied Lemnos
> of its males: we murdered every

one.

> And so
> it shall be here ... (l. 887)

she reminds herself, allowing Agamemnon to overhear her speaking to herself, her tongue tasting the me, as it often seemed—would come through. I didn't ask performers how the mo(ti)ves I'd shown them suited them, what other mo(ti)ves my mo(ti)ves suggested; I didn't want or need to know. Later, I did. My entire understanding of the interaction that takes place between choreographer/director and performer/interpreter during rehearsal changed, as did the work. And that is why I find myself thinking about Hamlet with his cover story and his covert stories as I attempt to understand my own covert story and the cover stories I have sometimes made up when asked to describe my work. But I'm not ready to drop Hamlet yet. I want first to take you back to rotting Denmark for the enactment of his piece.)

"The Mousetrap," Hamlet is to call it, when asked. And only when asked, I might add, for the curious delay in naming the work suggests that he was holding the name in reserve, waiting for the perfect moment to reveal it— or else that he had not yet settled on a title when it came time for his performance to begin, that he had still not chosen from among the myriad "working titles" that would have, oh, they surely must have, crossed his

words as she forms them and her ears testing his (in)credulity. She is developing a plan, a plot, and she is certain he will not stop her from carrying it out. How quickly she works now that she is in possession of an "idea." She need not take it through an arduous rehearsal process at the end of which it may be transformed beyond recognition; she merely acts: she seeks out Polymestor, pretends that she knows nothing of his crime, that she wishes to reward him and his sons for caring for young Polydorus,[4] that they need only follow her to a secret place within the female prisoners' quarters, that they would find there the gold and jewels she had hidden from marauding Greek soldiers; she knows that Polymestor and his sons will follow her; she knows, too, that they will find not gold and jewels, but the women of Troy, who will flatter them, praise their fine looks, their fine clothes and lances; she knows that Polymestor and his sons will hardly notice that the women have disarmed them; she wonders if Polymestor will have closed his eyes, allowing himself to fall into a state midway between waking and dreaming, when the women of Troy take out their brooches and stab them into those eyes that were so looking forward to the sight of gold, if his sons will have a moment to reflect on mind before the curtain opened, and that he might have left the work untitled had the question not been posed to him, or might have titled it differently, depending on how it was posed, on who did the posing—though in the postmodern manner, he will deny authorship. "The story is extant" (III, ii, 252), Hamlet declares; "and written in a very choice Italian," he adds, leaving even the translation uncredited, meanwhile introducing an element of foreign intrigue, a saucy, Mediterranean flavor to his theatrical offering by calling attention to its Italian source. Indeed, Hamlet has constructed the work he comes to call "The Mousetrap" in quite the postmodern manner. The way he interpolates new material into a "found" text (the "extant" story, "The Murder of Gonzago") so as to update it, make it more immediately relevant to its intended audience; or the way he stages the story twice, first in pantomime and then in verse, switching genres without transition; or the way he repeatedly interrupts the action to address the spectators directly:[4] do not these directorial strategies, this taste for complication, seem familiar, contemporary? They are in fact techniques with a long and varied history. The gap between our time and Hamlet's—or rather, Shakespeare's, for the time has surely come to name

how their father chose this fate for them after the women of Troy have pierced their hearts with hidden daggers. She trusts the Trojan women with their "hands which never held a sword" (l. 1032) to carry out her plan. And they do not let her down, these Trojan women soon to board a slave ship bound for Greece, each with her own secret reason for participating in the plot, her own cover(t) story which exile will transform. Hecuba is proud of their collective work:[5]

Watch him as he stumbles and staggers out of the tent
stone-blind.
See the bodies of his sons,
killed by my women and me

His debt is paid
And I have my revenge (l. 1050)

What Hecuba may not have realized is that in taking from this violent, vain and avaricious man his sight, she gave to him the gift of second sight, of seeing's double, and that if second sight be deemed a gift, she did perhaps reward him, after all.[6] Or did she? Would not she, Cassandra's mother, have known that visionary eyes could be a cruel curse?

Now something in the air was stirring, through not yet the wind that would allow Greek ships to him, the one who turned "extant story" into unforgettable tragedy—is indeterminate in extent, neither as vast nor as small as one imagines, both vaster and smaller.

travel homeward with the Trojan captives. And now blind Polymestor, suddenly a kind of prophet, turns his newly visionary eyes to face the face belonging to the woman who had caused his transformation. He tells her of a metamorphosis she's soon to undergo, how she will turn into a dog, become "a bitch with blazing eyes" (l. 1265)—but of course he would mention the eyes!—and how the bitch on board the slave ship will become deranged, will climb the masthead, fall to sea and drown. And so emboldened is he by the new and strange prophetic sound of his own voice that he adds one more prediction: that no one will retrieve her body, that her canine remains will be left to decompose in straits that will forever be known as *Cynossema*, bitch's grave, a landmark for sailors, a danger remark.

Hecuba "spits" on the prophecy with her reply: "What do I care how I die" (l. 1274). There is (n)either belief (n)or disbelief in these words. Having spoken them, she has come to the cessation of caring, and the tale of which she is the central character—an "extant story" given tragic form by Euripides; the time has surely come for me to name him—is over.

And what of the actor who, centuries later, would recite Aeneas' speech at Hamlet's request? Did the tears that fell from his eyes recall the noble suffering of the queen or the ignoble suffering of the slave, or—is "suffering" the word for it?—of the dog, the bitch, the beast, the monster?

And the actor playing the part of the player, what personal material, what image, what muscular memory is he summoning to generate the tears that Hamlet envies and abhors—

Over, but not done with.

Aeneas, who escaped from burning Troy before these gruesome events occurred, would not have known the fate of Queen Hecuba when he spoke of her, of the great suffering she endured, to Queen Dido—who would find the teller of the tale alluring, and would come to know great suffering because of that allurement.

Tears for Hecuba.

Many have wept for these characters. I have. Have you? They are truly magnificent creations, and they are due some sacrificial offering. One offers one's tears.

But the moments I have highlighted in their dramas are not the moments that wring tears out of eyes—though, perhaps, they could be, had I presented them differently. I've presented them as reflective moments, "self-reflexive," even. They are moments—and they occur, such moments, in the most action-packed dramas—when action is impeded. Reflection impedes action, halts narrative, disrupts fluidity, and it can make the one who witnesses it—the spectator—the "you"—you, for example, whom I've addressed from time to time as I've been writing—as uneasy with self-awareness as the character whose consciousness is on alert.

More than "characters" it is the fluctuations in (and out of) the consciousness of the figure on stage that I watch for, listen for, wait for when some kind of drama is unfolding before me, even the most action-packed drama. (And the dramas I have been [re]considering are action-packed, though each in vastly different ways. Shakespeare, a man of his time, put the action on stage, in the spectators' faces. *Hamlet* could be a TV special, a report on the decadent rich to titillate middle class fantasies of their lives. For Euripides, a man of his time, violent acts were not portrayed on stage; they were reported by messengers; what one saw and heard were the effects on the characters whom they befell. How terrifying an actor's exit must have been for those in attendance, who knew, and didn't know what was destined to occur in that invisible realm. *Hecuba* could not, would not be televised). And this brings me to my cover story, my after-the-fact explanation for why I've been where I've been as a choreographer: Where dance (like drama) traditionally has shown action interrupted by, punctuated by, moments of reflection, I've followed the opposite strategy, compiling reflective moment upon reflective moment, occasionally disrupting the near-static tableaus with flurries of movement, using dance to demonstrate the absence of dance—or has that been my alibi, my explanation for why I haven't been where I could have been? . . . I mean . . . words fail me.

Notes for Hamlet column

Notes for Hecuba column

1   "Wandering actors, like wandering homosexuals, are dangerous because they threaten to expose the fiction of stable homes," writes Peggy Phelan in "Playing Dead in Stone" (*Performance and Cultural Politics*, ed. Elin Diamond, London and New York: Routledge, 1996, 73).

2   Compare to Hamlet's words these of Antonin Artaud in *The Theater and its Double* (trans. M.C. Richards. New York: Grove Press, 1958):

"The state of the victim who dies without material destruction, with all the stigmata of an absolute and almost abstract disease upon him, is identical with the state of an actor entirely penetrated by feelings that do not benefit or even relate to his real condition. Everything in the physical state of the actor, as in that of the victim of the plague, shows that life has reacted to the paroxysm, and yet nothing has happened" (24).

or,

"The theater must make itself the equal of life—not an individual life, that individual aspect of life in which CHARACTERS triumph, but the sort of liberated life which sweeps away human individuality and in which man is only a reflection" (116).

Yet Shakespeare disappointed Artaud:

1   My speculations on Hecuba are based on William Arrowsmith's translation of the play in *Euripides III* (ed. David Greene and Richard Lattimore. New York: Washington Square Press, 1970).

2   Writing on the metapsychology of the survivor, Elias Canetti describes "[h]ow the craving for invulnerability and the passion for survival merge into each other" (*Crowds and Power*, trans. Carol Stewart. New York: Farrar Straus Giroux, 1984, 443). There is a difference between having *witnessed* the death of everyone that matters—losing "everything but life" and *feeling oneself to be dead* as well (as in Hecuba's case)—in contrast to having wished for the death of everyone that matters, and feeling oneself to be immortal (in Judge Schreber's case, which Canetti is discussing); yet the non-parallel lines converge at a point one must force oneself to imagine.

3   Herbert Golder comments: "Hecuba's vivid description of highly stylized tragic acting find many comparable parallels in descriptions of what these later writers all dancing, from skill at 'speaking with hands through gesture' to the ability to assume a range of intelligible or powerfully evocative postures, or schemata. In other words, this so-called dancing bears striking resemblance to a stylized form of acting and possibly even the genius and genesis of tragedy" ("Making a Scene: Gesture, Tableau, and the Tragic

"If, in Shakespeare, a man is sometimes preoccupied with what transcends him, it is always in order to determine the ultimate consequences of this preoccupation within him, i.e., psychology" (77).

3   In "Street Talk," Avital Ronell discusses the phantom in what she calls "Shakespeare's great rumor text":

"Hamlet is organized around a concept of a nothing and nowhere that speaks. The sense of drama and the source of information it gives about itself issue from a form of nothing . . . as origin of all rumors is the ghost, of course. The phantom utterance itself originates from something that resembles the transmission of a rumor text. For we must not forget that Hamlet's father dies of a poison that was poured into his ear, and the whole drama recycles this poison, from mouth to ear in a great ring of espionage and infection (separated, like Polonius, only by a curtained membrane). Infecting and paralyzing everybody, including the body politic, rumor, whose only paternity is the ghost of paternity (Heidegger: 'It's beyond me'), is the very thing that Hamlet wants confirmed. And so the ghost transmits a poisoned paternity to which every ear is open" (*Finitude's Score: Essays for the End of the Millennium*. Lincoln and London: University of Nebraska Press, 1994, 95).

5   Ophelia's comment on Hamlet's continual interference with the production is both insightful and provocative: "You are as good as a chorus, my lord" (III, ii, 236).

Chorus," *Arion, A Journal of Humanities and the Classics,* Vol. 4, no. 1:9).

4   In *The Fragility of Goodness*, Martha Nussbaum highlights this scene, writing as follows: "The most horrible thing about betrayal is that the person does look the same. He is identical with the person she has loved. She cannot help being moved; but she knows that she must not be moved. If once she looks at those eyes that open to contain her, then her hope of safety is gone. She is his relatum, his eyes' creature. She is, above all, what he sees when he sees her. Given the nature of his vision, that would make her nothing . . . . 'Don't think it's bad feeling about you, Polymestor,' [Hecuba] tells him. She knows, we see, that she is telling him the truth, as well as lying" (Cambridge: Cambridge University Press, 1986, 411–13).

5   Always giving and unforgiving with his intelligence, Herbert Blau writes of "Euripides who, with an instinct for the otherness that could not be kept in the dark, intensified the questions, as if he'd taken the opening into time, and looked on the face of the future . . . . He looked upon the future, and it was not an inspiriting prospect. Foreseeing as he did the end of the Athenian empire, he also gave us an image of collectivity as either a function of brutalizing power or the millenary prospect of inherited myth, which might be, with ample evidence in our century, no closing like access to the unconscious, with some eventual dilation of abscess of closure when—in a body without organs,

Rereading the line, it takes on various meanings: how "good" is the chorus, really? with how many voices in how many different registers does Hamlet speak? how classically grounded is his dramaturgy?

upswelling with desire—the unconscious seems to assume the contours of the crowd" (*The Audience*. Baltimore: Johns Hopkins University Press, 1990, 369). I wonder how Blau thinks his way through the fact that these collectivities tend to be gendered female in Euripides' drama.

6 It's worth pursuing this line of thought a bit further—to the next stop, the next station—with Jacques Derrida, who writes the following meditation on blindness in *Memoirs of the Blind*. He writes of it as possibly being "a blessing, a prize, a reward, a divine 'requital,' the gift of poetic and political clairvoyance, the chance for prophecy. There is nothing marvelous or astonishing in this: [Andrew] Marvell believed he knew that in losing his sight man does not lose his eyes. On the contrary. Only then does man begin to think the eyes. His own eyes are not those of just any animal" (trans. Pascale-Anne Brandt and Michael Naas. Chicago: University of Chicago Press, 1993, 1289).

—1997

commentary

IMAGE

From an immurement beneath layers and layers of invisibly suspended, blue-black gauze comes a faint sound—we cannot be certain if it is whimper or whisper—only breath, really, making the gauze itself seem to breathe, undulate ever so slightly, dimple, bow, dimple, bow. Within these layers, so it is rumored, lies a woman, supine, on a wooden pallet. Down the center of the pallet is said to run a prickly furrow of furze, tickling and irritating her spine. It is further rumored that, from time to time, in a fit of heartbreak and obstinacy, she rocks, faster and faster from side to side, until she has achieved a deafening ululating pitch emanating from what would be, if we were able to see her, a densely construed, fecund blur of blinding light.

REFLECTION

We may seize upon Marjorie Gamso's "Cover(t) Stories" as an illustration of the difference between brain and mind: The parallel construction may be read as left and right hemispheres, the space between them analogous to the corpus callosum, the band that separates the brain's two halves while simultaneously allowing connections to be made; mind, unable to be physically located, and difficult to define, encompasses that which may or may not be intended. Perusing Gamso's text, there is an underlying message whose presence begins to be sensed "behind the arras."[1]

"Cover(t) Stories," is, as its title suggests, encoded. It is an obliquely passionate and grieving text, "a complicated tale,"[2] indicated not only by Gamso's choice of characters and structure, but by what lies buried within its apparent narrative. A specific form of loss is identified, as stinging as that of innocence or purity, to which it bears a resemblance: it is the loss of the fleet and fleeing initial impulse, or *inspiration*. So frustrating is this provisional control over the initial idea in relation to subsequent changes, and so laborious the process of mounting a finished piece that, despite the dire situations of the two protagonists Gamso has chosen, it induces a certain envy: "[Hamlet] is possessed of an 'idea'," and commensurately, "[Hecuba] is in possession of an 'idea'."[3] Neither of them need "*take it through an arduous rehearsal process at the end of which [these ideas] may be transformed beyond recognition*"[4] (italics mine).

Gamso is thus able to find desirable a condition common to both Hamlet and Hecuba, and which confirms its opposite: the sorrow of finding oneself farther and far-

ther removed from the moment of inspiration, a moment which might also be perceived as making contact with a unified self before that self begins to fragment, and disappear from view. The initial moment is "pure," asserting itself momentarily before
self-reflection, or the self-reflexive, is set in motion. It is the "monstrousness" of transformation that proves debilitating, its origins no longer able to be read, no longer synchronous with self; it is beyond our control. The idea will not speak to us directly any
longer, as it spoke its initial utterance to its solitary witness. The monster—the project—
begins to grow(l). It is compelling to try and stalk it back to its lair. A struggle ensues,
an attempt to recoup the impulse .

Gamso, who at first is front and center, alludes to this in her opening paragraph
before she retreats from view in the ensuing activity, as in the smoke and disarry of a
Trojan battle. Surfacing 'as herself' now and again before reappearing, alone and overtly, at the end of the text, she details what happens when "Movement phrases . . . begin to
change," citing two highly emotional states experienced in trying to recapture them:
"feverish and hysterical," and two more, "futile and hilarious," the latter of which are, by
scant degree, slightly more distanced for being nominally after the fact.

Continuing to move into Gamso's parallel text, it might be paraphrastically asked,
what's Hamlet or Hecuba to Gamso? Why these particular choices? An answer may be
found in "Cover(t) Stories" play of passion(s)-*cum*-Passion play: Gamso uses these tales of
tragedy and misfortune, in some measure, to elucidate her own project: Hamlet, seemingly more in control, the more behavioristic, externalized stand-in in regard to organiz-
ing and naming his production; Hecuba as surrogate for an internalized state ocurring as
the result of being a woman thwarted as she urgently tries to be heard, understood.
Shakespeare, while giving credence to science and the psychological, referenced, among
other sources and influences, Greek and Roman classics, astrology, ghosts, and witchcraft,
rather than advancing a particularly Christian point of view; Euripides' Greece was pre-
Christian and polytheistic. Still, Gamso's text can be read as syncretic; it implies that art-
making, if not actual martyrdom, is punishment, an unrecognized calling (out), a
"Remember me,"[5] a request, a plea, unable to be either reconciled or abandoned. Gamso
began her choreographic project almost three decades ago, a stringently conceptual artist
in a form and milieu associated, in the West, with movement flow, which Gamso's work
most definintely and defiantly has never been nor become. Her choreography, though
changed—more emotive—retains structural elements of these conceptualist influences
and principles, such as the repetition and stillness found in her earlier work.

There is a tension in Gamso's textual strategy: the classical weight of the references under current consideration does not dismiss her text's sensuality, its heart and heat and, concurrently, does not diminish its use as smokescreen, subterfuge, a diversion which seemingly covers up Gamso personally, and renders the text, whether intentionally (consciously) or, at times, guilelessly (unconsciously) a construct, a mousetrap, or in her case, a game of hide and seek: now you see "I," now you don't. "I've been through this routine, and I am now thinking.... No, I will let you in on what Hamlet is thinking... "[6] It is this desire to simultaneously display and hide that provokes the tension. As if on intimate terms with these characters, she has 'interviewed' them, is giving us the scoop. It is bagged intellectual quarry, posed beside, yet shorn of posturing. Aware of our presence, hopeful enough to assume as much, Gamso is performing for us, speaking to us, knowing we are here.

Gamso makes use of masks, the ability of the written word to cross-dress at will, externalize an internal dialogue carried on with, or on behalf of, characters, male or female and, by implication, their long-dead creators, as well as more recent sources cited in her footnotes. Gamso's text is an entertainment, aware of both its poetic and didactic possibilities. The spectator/reader's attention is arrested by the structure and maintained, in part, through the aforementioned personalizing device, the diving-and-surfacing effect created by inserting the "I" now and again, and the sensuousness of references to tongues, eyes, ears, those organs that bring the world to us as inspiration before the mind transforms them into their ever-fragmenting, shattered and shattering meanings. The moments when Gamso appears, between the framing that occurs at the beginning and end, is a 'mirror image' of a stripper removing garments a bit a time. It is the purported secret we find seductive, whether of flesh or mind.

Though Gamso claims that, in the end, "[W]ords fail [her]," it is their medium that has provided material. Despite empathy for the characters she has chosen to examine, she retains her particularity, her human, nonfictive identity; she is not—fortunately, and most certainly with her compliance—poor, sad Queen Hecuba, "not Prince Hamlet, nor was meant to be."[7]

AFTERIMAGE

A woman curls the fingers of her right hand, one after the other, as though closing a fan; her eyes dart left and her head turns slightly in the same direction as though sensing a shadowy figure standing just beyond a circle of light on the darkest night in memory.

notes

1   William Shakespeare, *Hamlet, Prince of Denmark* (New York: Pocket Books, 1992), 173.

2   "Cover(t) Stories," 66.

3   Ibid., 68/72.

4   Ibid., 72.

5   Ibid., 70.

6   Ibid., 68.

7   T.S. Eliot, "The Love Song of J. Alfred Prufrock," *Collected Poems, 1909–1962, The Centenary Edition* (New York: Harcourt Brace, 1968), 7.

John Kelly, front
Ishmael Houston-Jones, back
Photo: Tom Brazil

three texts

ishmael houston-jones

the annotated end
of everything

I APPROACH PUTTING WORDS ON THE PAGE
in much the same way that I approach
finding movement for the stage. My best
writing is like my best dancing—
instinctive, improvised and free flowing.
I started using spoken text in my dances around 1977, when I first saw Trisha
Brown's speaking/dancing solo *Accumulation with Talking.* Although it was very
different from anything I would ever make, I loved seeing and hearing Trisha keep
switching back and forth between two stories and two dances. My own first experiments combining the two media left me stuck in a story telling mode. The work
was really literal: it wasn't writing for performance. Then I began to reduce the writing to its essence until finally there was nothing left but lists of words. No adjectives
or description of any kind. Just words slamming, bumping or nestling against each
other. Any color had to come from the context of being placed between the word
that came before and the one that would come after. In *D E A D*—which I performed for my thirtieth birthday in 1981—I improvised a list of every death, real
or imagined, that I could remember happening in my lifetime, while I fell to and

rose from the floor repeatedly, in a simple dance of exhaustion:

De Gaulle / Piaf / Malcolm X / Helen Keller / Sid Vicious

In "*Part 2: Relatives*" (1982) I began with a long spinning dance performed while trying to recall the first names of my ancestors from my great-great-grand parents onward. When I collaborated with the writer Dennis Cooper on *THEM,* in 1985, he included two list pieces of his own—"10 Dead Friends" and "10 Bedded Friends"—in his script.

In time, the purity of writing only lists began to feel like a constricting limitation. I wanted to tell more of a narrative than could be told by merely placing word next to word next to word. In 1988 I wrote a short story titled "Prologue to the End of Everything." The list structure survived but now it existed as short chapters of numbered sentences and phrases. Set in an unnamed, plague-riddled, war-torn tropical Hell, it reads like a slide show of the sexual nightmares of Matt, the protagonist.

Commissioned by the Kitchen in New York, I set about turning this short story into an evening length dance. The piece was made in close collaboration with composer Chris Cochrane, photographer Robert Flynt, and performers Trinket Monsod and Antaney Bowman. Hanging sculptures were by Impala, lighting by Michael Stiller and additional music was provided by Zeena Parkins and Doug Seidel.

Our task was to deconstruct an already fractured narrative in order to get to the core of Matt's world. He was a marooned stranger in a land where the horror of violence and the excitement of sex merged; where furtive love making was always a prelude to possible death. The story, as written, was ripped open. Large sections were deleted. Various devices were used such as having voices taped, or miked live, or spoken in canon. Dance improvisations were structured around the text and music score.

What follows is the text for the opening solo (in bold type) with my own notes about what the structure of the accompanying dance might be in normal typeface. I performed this solo—apart from the rest of the piece—for a year, as part of the P.S. 122 Field Trips, the touring program of Performance Space 122. The movement for the piece was not "set" in the traditional choreographic sense, but as it was performed repeatedly definite themes and landmarks emerged in response to the text. I've watched two different versions of the opening solo on video tape to help with my annotations.

PROLOGUE TO THE END OF EVERYTHING

The piece begins with a music overture, and slides. The slides, by Robert Flynt, are projections of fully clothed people floating under water. After the slides are over, the white fabric on which they were being shown is lowered. The stage is black. The sound of something slapping against the floor can be heard in the darkness. Slowly a small circle of cold, blue-white light fades up, upstage right, to reveal a man dressed in a gray sleeveless undershirt, short gray military pants and combat boots, obsessively beating the floor with a white formal dress shirt. He is looking down. When he stops, he stands waving the shirt in front of his face as though he were trying to signal a rescue ship or plane. He turns upstage, still without revealing his face. He slips into the shirt, which is several sizes too large for him. The cuffs almost cover his fingertips. With his back to the audience he gestures and says, live:

The airport had been closed for almost a week; there was a ban on exit visas; Matt sleeps and dreams of women in damp blouses, denim skirts and pink plastic sandals;

Backlit, he turns slowly toward the audience and brushes "dust" from his shirt and shorts.

of Iguanas calling him from a vacant lot;

With both hands above his head he makes shadow puppets of iguanas talking.

of strawberries the size of babies' red fists.

Supporting his right elbow in his left hand, his right hand is in a fist that he twists and admires.

He dreams of sucking on ice cubes,

Hand in mouth.
and the busboy's eyelashes.

Hands flutter like birds from his face out toward the audience.
Standing, legs together, he rhythmically taps his left wrist with his right

fingertips as if trying to get a malfunctioning watch to work.
From this point on, the text is a taped voice-over.

1. He wakes up, a wrestler defeated by his own sweaty sheet.

Brings wrist to ear, listening for ticking.

2. He wakes up, reassured by the sounds of lizards on his screens and parrots in the trees.

Resumes tapping his wrist.

3. He wakes up, takes a piss in a green, plastic bucket,

He slaps the insides of both thighs and opens legs and arms to a wide second position squat. He looks back and forth from thigh to thigh.

takes a short look at two unhealing sores, spits out some red foamy toothpaste, rinses his mouth with rum,

Stands again with legs together he resumes rhythmically tapping his left wrist with his fingers, perhaps with a little more desperation.

takes a painful, watery, rotten-eggy shit, checks for blood,

Listens to "wrist watch" again.

sprinkles some pine oil into the bucket.

Again slaps the insides of both thighs, opens legs and arms to a wide, second-position plié. Slowly rotates one arm, then the other palm skyward.

4. Matt heads for the café.
He never liked this café.
It's in the "bourzhie" quarter across from the Palace Hotel.
It's the only one that's still open.

Staying in second-position plié he circles one arm around his head as if wiping sweat or winding on a turban. He continues this over the next six lines, slowly working his feet together to a standing position.

5. He steps over a few new bodies.

6. The heat is bearable, but just.

7. His toes curl under, inside his boots.

8. There are more bodies than yesterday.

9. And a few left over from the day before.

10. The squads are getting sloppy.
   Or overworked.

Stands facing stage left, profile to audience.

11. He gets to the Palace.

Right arm outstretched toward audience.

12. The same woman and little girl are begging on the corner.

13. The woman is dead.

With arm still outstretched pivots slowly toward audience.

14. The girl holds a cup. Stares straight ahead.

15. A sign in her language is taped to her T-shirt.

Pounds chest very hard three times over next line.

16. It reads —"Blessed Mother, protect my precious one."

Left hand extended to the side, palm down, hand opening and closing rapidly as the right arm is extended forward, palm up, fingers beckoning.

17. He drops some sweat-crumpled bills into the cup.

18. About twenty-five and a half cents, U.S.

19. The girl doesn't say thank you, not even automatically.

20. He thinks, this is unusual, he thinks.

21. He thinks—she'll probably be dead by nightfall.

He turns in profile to the audience and begins a "mosquito-swatting dance" over the next nine lines, rhythmically "swatting" his forehead, shoulder, and thigh.

22. At the café, his favorite waitress tells him a nephew died last evening.

23. That's four people in her family this month.

24. He expresses his sorrow and orders a rum.

25. He orders a rum.

26. There's an attractive university student reading Franz Fanon at the next table.

27. There are listless parrots in huge cages.

28. There's the busboy he always overtips.

29. He orders a rum.

30. He orders a rum.

Abruptly faces audience. Two fingers of right hand in the air.

This one with a bottle of Coke,

Right hand, palm out, in the "stop" position.

with the cap still on please.
And he adds needlessly—

Right forefinger "cuts his throat."

of course without ice.

31. He strains to see the headlines on the cute student's newspaper.

Gives a "Heil Hitler" straight arm salute with right arm.

32. Death toll, as always, in the upper right corner,

Left arm swings upward and to side, with palm facing upward.

and assurances that scientific help is coming from the outside.

Demurely lifts hem of shorts.

A message from the First Lady.

Turns stage left profile.

Something about the World Futbol Cup.

In profile, begins a series of jumps over the next seven lines. Jumps by kicking himself in the ass with both feet at once while at the same time bending arms so that fists touch shoulders. Lands by stomping loudly and extending arms downward. (An alternative over these seven lines is to run in place.)

33. And a factory nearby that manufactures binary chemical weapons has been taken over by . . .

34. But the attractive student's nose has begun to bleed.

35. Badly.

36. And people are running down the street past the Palace Hotel.
    Ripping up shrubbery.
    Throwing paving stones.

37. It's a lot like TV.

38. The waitress gives the attractive student a kitchen rag and tilts his
    head back.

39. More people are running screaming in the streets.

He turns his body upstage and looks back over his right shoulder at audience.
He extends his right buttock, then touches his right buttock with his right hand.

40. The parrots wake up to beat their wings against the bars of their cages.

Pats right butt cheek.

41. He hears what could be firecrackers or gunshots or mortar fire and he
    thinks he really should learn the difference.

Mouths the following quote along with taped voice.

42. He thinks out loud—"What I should do is get my black ass back to
    New York and fast."

43. Paving stones are being thrown at the café.
    Tables overturned.

He turns to face audience, extending his right arm forward. He begins a series
of turns over the next six lines in which the right arm leads the body in a half-
turn to the right, then the left arm leads the body one-quarter turn to the left.

44. The busboy says, "Follow me, you'll be safe," and leads him into the walk-in box.

45. All he can hear is the sound of the motor.
    All he can feel is cool air.
    All he can smell is fresh clean blood.

46. The busboy says in his language, "We'll be safe here."

47. The busboy sticks his tongue in his mouth.

48. Matt thinks of Elizabeth's latest letter asking why he doesn't come home and take that teaching job.

49. The busboy unbuttons Matt's pants, pulls them down and spins him around 180° .

At the last half-turn to the right the man arrives facing upstage, arms frozen overhead in the "stick 'em up" position.

50. He thinks of his father teaching him to ride a two-wheeler.

With his back to the audience he waves his arms as if signaling for help. Or reaching for support.

51. He supports himself holding onto the cold slimy carcasses of two calves hanging from meat hooks—skinny as dogs.

His legs are wobbly. He alternates being a member of the ground crew guiding a jet to the terminal and being a slowly collapsing marionette.

52. He hears the busboy's pants unzip behind him and he thinks of paintings by Francis Bacon.

53. The busboy slaps his ass.

Music begins under text. (Sample of Egyptian clay drums.)

54. **He hears a loud explosion out beyond the heavy metal door and the cool.**
    More screams.
    More breaking glass.
    More parrot squawks and firecrackers.

55. **"Your legs are very beautiful but what are those marks?" asks the busboy in his language.**

With his back to the audience he begins unbuttoning his shirt.

56. **"It's the end," Matt answers.**

57. **Then, "No, it's not the end."**

Music of electric guitar and harp begins to drown out text.

58. **His fingers dig into the fat and muscle of the two hanging calves.**

Turning to face the audience, he skins off his shirt and uses it to wipe his brow.

59. **The busboy orders, "Relax!"**

He tosses the dress shirt to the floor.

60. **It's not the end.**
    It's the beginning.
    The beginning of the end of everything.

Begins improvising the opening dance with the musicians. The dance takes place in a narrow channel of light. Movement imagery may come from the text that was just heard or from words that will come later in the piece. Or the dance may be a visceral response to the hard edge of the music or the ghostliness of the photographs of the "drowned" men.

—1997

score for *D E A D*

D E A D is a solo dance/performance piece created June 8, 1981, as part of a celebration of my thirtieth birthday.

A. On the evening before performing the dance, prerecord a list of every death I can remember which has occurred during my lifetime. Allow pauses for memory lapses. Even if I am not sure a death happened in the last thirty years, if it seems like a real death in the moment, I must say it. Allow for people and pets I've known personally; relatives of people I've known; deaths of celebrities I've experienced through the news media; and fictional characters whose deaths seem real to me at the time.

B. On the day of performance play the tape.

C. For the first three or four names stand still and as I hear each name make the American Sign Language sign for "DEAD" (i.e., left hand open with palm facing downward and right hand open with palm facing upward. Turn both hands over so that they are in the opposite orientation from their starting positions).

D. When I hear a name that has a particular resonance for me, fall down to the floor in some emblematic way and try to rise again before the next name is called. As the next, and the next, and then the next names are spoken, repeat the falling to the floor and rising dance for each name.

E. Try not to anticipate a death. Try not to remember the death until I hear myself speak it on the tape. Try to respond to the death in the moment. Try to let go of the death as I rise from the floor.

F. Continue until there are no more names, (about ten minutes). Allow myself to become exhausted with the effort. Don't stop until the dance is over.

JFK * RFK * Martin Luther King * Fred Hampton * Field Marshall Cinque * Jim Jones *************** Kitty Genovese ********************* Grandma Shadwick *** Grandpa Shadwick ************ Aunt Sister *** Uncle Son

***************************** Adrian ***** James ***** Charlie Jones ********** Jones, Charles H. USMC ************** Cathy Noland *** Nick Adams *** Monty *** Jean Seberg ********* John 23 *** Paul 6 *** John Paul 1 ********************* LBJ *** Hubert Humphrey *** Martha Mitchell *** Judy Garland *** Hop-a-long Cassidy *** Jacques Brel *** Phil Ochs *************************** Rango *** Nugget the First *** Nugget the Second *** Zincy ******** Roy Campanella *** Joe Louis *** Ezra Charles *** Emile Griffith *********************** Bob Crane *** Sal Mineo **** Clark Gable **** Marilyn ************ Patrice Lumumba ****** Joseph Kasavubu ********* All eight except Corazón Amuro *************** Jack Ruby *** Joe Kennedy ****** Franco *** Eichmann ********* Gary Gilmore ***** Reza Pahlavi ******** Ike *** Mamie ********************* Warren's mother *** Warren's father *** Jeff's grandmother *** Kathy's sister *** Larry's dog *** Ginsberg's mother *** Ginsberg's father ********** Jim Morrison ****** Jimi Hendrix ****** Gus Grissom **** Janis Joplin **** Gracie Allen *********** Jack Benny *********** Spanky ***** Charlie Chaplin *** The man who used to sing on Jackie Gleason *** One of the Rolling Stones *** John Lennon ********* Maria Callas ********* Queen Fredericka **** King Paul *** The Duke of Windsor *** Duke Ellington *********************** John Wayne **** Superman **** Lassie ***** Ramón Navarro ********* Patsy Cline ***** Michael Bloomfield ******** Sharon Percy *** Sharon Tate ********** Inge Stevens ****** Jayne Mansfield ****************** Bess and Harry Truman ********************De Gaulle/Piaf/Malcolm X/Helen Keller/Sid Vicious ********************* two at Jackson State ******************** four at Kent State *** A lot at My Lai ******* Less than a thousand at Jonestown *********************** Wil Johnnson *** Charles Geary ***** Manya Starkman *** Miss Kunkel ******** Wally Cox * James Dean * Ernie Kovacs * Joan Crawford * Khrushchev * Dag Hammarskjöld * Madam Nu's husband * Louis Armstrong * Golda Meir.

—1981

a dance of identity: notes
on the politics of dancing

I first used the form *The Politics of Dancing* in 1986 as a rehearsal tool while working on *Adolfo und Maria*, a piece with a large multi-ethnic cast, which dealt with the complicity of the artist in the racism and fascism of governments. I needed to get fourteen people to really look at and work with one another. Earlier that year I had had a conversation with choreographer Liz Lerman about art/political work she was doing in Washington, D.C. She described a performance there—I can't remember if it was an actual event or just a proposal—at which audience members were given three cards. They would receive either black or white cards depending upon responses to questions placing them inside or outside American dominant culture. The three categories were sex, race, and sexual orientation. Since the classification for this performance assumed male Caucasian heterosexuals to be dominant in our society, straight white men would receive three white cards while black lesbians would receive three black ones. Those who had some dominant traits, but not all, would get two of one color and one of the other. My memory of what Liz described was that the audience was then seated in four sections of the hall, based upon how many white cards they had: three, two, one or none. With Liz's description of this performance vivid in my memory, I began rehearsals.

I wanted something more multi-faceted that would address the more elusive ways in which people perceive others and make assumptions about what those perceptions might mean. I wanted to explore some of the subtle and not so subtle ways people act upon those perceptions and assumptions. I also wanted people to feel what it was like to be in a minority facing a much larger group. I was interested to know which groupings caused people discomfort, which ways they liked to be grouped, and when they would lie or resist the categorizing. I wanted to break down knee-jerk responses, and have people look beyond the superficial things they were seeing to find the origins of the responses they were having.

THE FORM AS IT FIRST EXSISTED:

The fantasy of *Adolfo und Maria* was that there was a troupe of minstrels performing in the cabarets of pre-World War II Germany. The entire cast was in blackface and, as in the tradition of both minstrel shows and cabaret, they performed skits of topical political satire. The main show was a burlesque about the German choreographer Mary Wigman and her dubious connection to Hitler, which culminated in her choreographing the opening ceremony of the 1936 Olympics for him.

I gathered the cast in a large clump in the center of the room, standing very near one another. I explained that we were on a railroad track and a train was approaching. I instructed that if you were a "MAN" you should go to one wall and form a group with the other men. If you were "NOT A MAN" you should go to the opposite wall and group with the others who were not men. What was key at this moment, and, as it turned out, most difficult, was that I wanted the two groups (the "MEN" and the "NOT MEN") to look at the members of their own group first and not back at the "others." I asked them to look for similarities and differences, to check themselves for expectations, assumptions, and surprises regarding the others with whom, by this one factor alone, they had been grouped. Since this was the first division, I allowed this inward looking at one's own group to take a longish amount of time. At a certain point I instructed the two groups to turn outward as a unit and to face and see the other group across the room; to see them as a mass, and as individuals, to look for the same things (differences, commonalities, etc.) as they had while looking inward. After a time, I had the two groups merge in the center of the room and divided them a different way, for example, "BLOND"/"NOT BLOND"; "HOMOSEXUAL"/"NOT HOMOSEXUAL"; "BOTH PARENTS LIVING"/"AT LEAST ONE PARENT DEAD." Besides going through the original check list of observations and responses, I now asked people to notice how each grouping felt compared to the ones that came before. Did one feel different about being one of eleven "RIGHT-HANDED" people looking across at three "LEFTIES" than one felt being one "ASIAN" woman looking across at thirteen "NON-ASIANS?" and if so, different in what way? The form allowed no extraneous talking or judgments—only observations and the emotional responses to them. We spent about forty-five minutes splitting apart, regrouping, then splitting apart again. We spent almost as much time afterwards discussing what it could all mean.

HOW THE FORM IS DEVELOPING

Over the years, I've led *The Politics of Dancing* in various contexts: workshops in U.S. colleges and European dance schools; at the Contact Teachers Conference in Berlin in 1988; as a rehearsal tool for other performance projects. I've heard that others who have done the form with me have gone on to lead it in workshops of their own. I've continued to develop the form, to try to deepen the possible meanings derived from doing it. The first major change was that I felt that I should no longer be the only one choosing the categories. I'd always felt manipulative and, in a sense, voyeuristic, eliciting personal information from the groups. I decided to give the first five or so instructions, and then invite another participant to continue for five, and then they would turn over the asking role to someone else. This almost inevitably led to a sort of round robin, group free-association of people randomly asking us to divide ourselves. I feel this is much more democratic, and gets to the core of what the concerns of the entire circle are. I've further refined the role of the asker by instructing that each of us should think of a categorization that would place us in the majority (but not include everyone), one that would place us in the extreme minority, and one that would split the group in equal parts. While this last adjustment took away some of the free-form randomness of letting anyone split the group whenever they felt an impulse to do so, (often in response to the previous division), it added focus to the choices made by the participants and clarified the reasons for doing the exercise.

Another change I made from those first rehearsals is that I merged *The Politics of Dancing* with improvisation work I had begun doing with eyes closed. In the eyes-closed work, I try to get people to stop using vision as a handicap: that is, relying upon the information one gets from sight to the impediment of the other senses. I had the initial group form with eyes closed so that the only clues to the identity of the others around us came through touch, smell, temperature, and so on. I then asked that the person making the category always phrase the statement using the words "I" or "my," and that the statement had to be true for her/him. If, for example, the statement "I AM AN ONLY CHILD," or "MY EYES ARE BROWN," was true for another person, they were instructed to stay in the center of the room with the person who spoke; if it was not true, they were told to go to the wall and form a group there. The railroad tracks were now situated in the center of the room so that there could be no possibility of waffling in the middle. People were instructed not to open their eyes until they had formed an inward-oriented group. When they opened their eyes they were guided to look for the same things as in the earlier incarnation of the exercise—that is, similarities, differences, feelings about being grouped with these people. We then continued as before, always with a discussion afterwards.

SOME THOUGHTS ABOUT *THE POLITICS OF DANCING* EXERCISE, ITS USEFULNESS AND SOME POSSIBLE
PITFALLS AS A TOOL FOR PINPOINTING IDENTITY AND PREJUDICE

In its original form, as a rehearsal tool for a specific piece with a large cast, it was a good and fast way to get a disparate group of people to work together and deal with the difficult material of the piece. Some of the more dramatic separations were used in the performance of *Adolfo und Maria*. For example, an ensemble dance was interrupted by a loud sound and the "WHITE" performers were separated from the "NOT WHITE" performers; then the piece continued.

From the start I observed a tendency for some people to situate themselves somewhere between the railroad tracks and the wall, sticking to the middle, not fully committing themselves to either category. Early on, I felt I had to address this because for the exercise to be most powerful, people needed to commit in the moment to being "THIS" and "NOT THAT," and to experience being looked at as "the other." As I explained to one student who was having trouble with one division, the secret police knocking on doors during the Third Reich were not so interested in the subtle grays of identity. Also, by not choosing at the moment of questioning, you are possibly denying a component of your identity, and you should examine why it is that you cannot declare this trait to be a part of who you are.

At its worst, *The Politics of Dancing* can become a kind of glib party game where people try to get the embarrassing "goods" on their friends. This seems to happen most often when the participants are all young (late teens, early twenties), and have known each other in some other, more formal, context over time. This has happened when I've taught workshops as a guest teacher within a college dance department, and in my improvisation class at the American Dance Festival. I think I could have avoided this rowdiness and lack of serious focus by giving it a more thoughtful preamble; perhaps by explaining Liz Lerman's description of the piece in D.C. as a source of the work. Putting the exercise in some sort of context seems to be a necessary responsibility of the workshop leader. This means being clear why you think this particular group of people would benefit from doing it and not just throwing it in as a kind of interesting workshop activity.

I do believe that this form can deepen one's sense of identity in several ways. It forces one to publicly declare aspects of the self that are taken for granted, or are not often acknowledged (perhaps even to oneself). Also, one gets the experience of being looked at as one of a group of people who "DO NOT WANT

TO HAVE CHILDREN," or "HAVE BEEN ARRESTED," or "HAVE PARENTS WHO ARE COLLEGE GRADS." While for myself, I have had no qualms with being grouped with other "NON-WHITES," or 'NON-HETEROSEXUALS," I usually am uneasy being grouped with "MEN," and I feel exposed being looked at with the group of "PEOPLE WITH DEAD FATHERS." I have found that I usually derive a certain comfort being in the extreme minority, whereas others find this to be unsettling.

The most vexing statement has been, "I BELIEVE THAT I AM IN THE MORE INTELLIGENT HALF OF THIS WORKSHOP." People have left the room or insisted upon being hit by the train based upon their feelings about that one. In one rehearsal with eight men, seven went to the side of "MORE INTELLIGENT," while only one declared himself to belong in the "NOT MORE INTELLIGENT" half. The statements "I CONSIDER MYSELF TALL," or "I THINK THAT I AM OVERWEIGHT" often produce two groups that look identical in terms of height and weight. Personal perceptions can be deceiving.

ANECDOTES

I often relate an experience I had in the early 1980s when doing a lecture-demonstration at Elders Share the Arts, a seniors' arts center in the Bronx. I began teaching the workshop using the voice of a nanny talking to very young children. I asked in a completely condecending tone, "If you can, could you try to lift your arms above your head?" This being a senior center with its own performing arts group, filled with vital, creative people who just happened to be over sixty-five, they all immediately thrust their arms in the air, giving me very quizzical looks, the point being that in my life in the downtown "po-mo" dance world, I rarely came into direct contact with older people, and my conception of "PEOPLE OVER SIXTY-FIVE" was that they were all virtual cripples who needed to have even very simple things painstakingly explained to them.

When leading this form at the European Dance Development Center in Holland, the workshop of twelve was made up of about six Germans. When someone said, "I AM NOT GERMAN," we split accordingly. When we opened our eyes to focus within our own group, one of our "NOT GERMAN[S]" said to a man standing with us, "Hey, you belong over there." He responded that he didn't because he was Austrian, and a rather heated discussion broke out.

Once, during the discussion, after having done The Politics of Dancing at Bennington College here in the U.S., one student was very upset because her best friend had gone to the "JEWISH" group. Her friend explained that one of her parents was Jewish so in that moment she felt, to be true to her identity, she had to go to that side. The friend continued to be agitated all the while, insisting that she felt neutral about Jews and Jewishness. Someone asked her if she would feel the same way if she had just discovered that her best friend was "BORN IN CANADA" or "METHODIST."

Defining sexuality takes quite a bit of finessing. In a single workshop, "I AM GAY," "I AM HOMOSEXUAL," "I AM QUEER," "I HAVE INTERCOURSE ONLY WITH PEOPLE OF MY OWN GENDER" and their "opposites" can each produce very different splits in one group. A person who can stand with "I AM HETEROSEXUAL," may find it impossible to do so with "I HAVE SEX ONLY WITH PEOPLE OF THE OPPOSITE GENDER," or even simply, "I AM STRAIGHT." It seems that the politics of gender and identity and language have produced an infinitely complex dance.

—1996

commentary

IMAGE

From sky-high speakers, in the shape of distended bellies of the pregnant and starving, blares forth an unbearable silence. A naked presence, bent kneed, open-mouthed, stands between them, regarding a desolate, empty space, cradling an erection or two, amid bouts of deep consciousness. "Look, I think it's playing fair," the presence weeps, "to warn you, to tell you. That." Where the presence presides, the taste is very sharp with knowing, with salted anxiety, with whatever fuels desire. Fade to bona fide sighing, amped and keening.

REFLECTION

Ishmael Houston-Jones's multiple texts in *Footnotes* speak unabashedly of an "I" and an "other," postulating, by implication and example, the I's potential for extrapolation into relationship with the other, while still retaining its complex integrity as a single integer. The writing explicates the use of individuated identity as a conscious and conscientious means by which to launch the self into identification with a larger social milieu. It observes the arbitrarily imposed boundaries between self and other and seeks to remove them by first distinctly and clearly defining them. The texts signal his regard for sociopolitical content in his performance work. Houston-Jones's writing functions as a report of process, of the attempt to release the inner voice, to make it accessible, available and externalized without hypocrisy, duplicity, or shame.

Houston-Jones's language in all three texts is written familiarly, informed but informal, seemingly casually spoken, aware of its vernacular structure's relationship to the favored tenets or operations of Houston-Jones's performing mode: "[His] best writing is like [his] best dancing—instinctive, improvised and free-flowing" (p.85).

Houston-Jones's texts elide the written/spoken/performative aspects of his overall project. "*The Annotated End of Everything,*" begins with the writer referencing an "I" as an explanatory presence, 'out from behind' a persona; it details the process Houston-Jones generally uses, and the historical progress of this, and former pieces, as they led to the initial and subsequent use of text in his live work. It then proceeds to a specific text, where Houston-Jones abuts the persona of Matt, the protagonist in the performance, with descriptions of movement done in relation to this text by the person whose name is Ishmael Houston-Jones. This device, and the specific description of locale, encourages the reader to imagine, to "see."

In "*Score for D E A D*" Houston-Jones uses a gambit similar to the preceding. In ". . . *D E A D*," however, he organizes specific information about this particular piece only, cluing the reader into his internal responses to the list of names that follow and which, in turn, clue Houston-Jones, the performer, into on-the-spot responses. Here, he relates, he has set up the task of remaining spontaneous, as if hearing the text for the first time each time, rather than anticipating. The particularity and specificity involved in the act of naming does nothing to negate the impression of Houston-Jones's egalitarianism; he announces the names of the famous, the unknown, the real, and the fictional, making, along the way, a point confirming the weight and substance we attribute to certain written characters; the wide-ranging choice of names introduces a playful aspect into his reportage of the sheer physical labor of the performance and the underlying seriousness of the subject. The choice of subject, death—for all but the fictive characters—is in itself an implicitly leveled field. The final clue, or cue, to the meaning of ". . . *D E A D*," comes in Houston-Jones's statement that by naming/calling to the dead, and physically responding, he is letting go of each; it is a collision between Houston-Jones and the floor beneath him, between remembrance and forfeiture.

In "*A Dance of Identity: Notes on The Politics of Dancing*," the title sums up and overtly expresses Houston-Jones's concerns: dance, identity, politics. This examination of I and other takes place in head-on, heads-up milieus. He enunciates methods—utilized originally in rehearsals, and in workshops—by which personal beliefs, including those which may not be conscious prior to the experience he delineates, can inform the self in the process of 'going public,' and which are, ultimately, meant to reflect degrees of commonality, or at least clarify the differences. In this instance, Houston-Jones uses his art as a carpenter does a hammer, or a surgeon a scalpel, in its functional capacity: ". . . *as a rehearsal tool* . . . it was a good and fast way to get a disparate group of people to work together . . . " (p. 100 italics, mine). The structure of the writing used to convey this information is conventional, the style both anecdotal and editorial. The "I" is also the "eye", as Houston-Jones recreates the various mise-en-scène, from rehearsals to workshops, in which he has utilized these tactics of public acquittal in airing privately held beliefs. Houston-Jones does not spare himself in the telling. He writes of the ways in which he finds himself most comfortable or most exposed, and relates an experience which shows him to be, at an earlier date, parochial in certain assumptions. It is an implicit part of Houston-Jones's project that he not be seen supporting a hierarchical paradigm. He goes on to take the technique itself to task, stating, "At its worst, [it] can become . . . a glib party game" (p.100).

Houston-Jones's writing represents two modes, the experimental and the descriptive. As stated previously, in neither case is it the language itself that strays from what we recognize as common usage. That is part of its subversion. It is so clearly 'the way people speak' that it is left to the content and context to disrupt the smooth flow of expectation. It is, overall, text that announces desire, either directly or by implication, whether the desire for clarity through speech, or communion through sex; it is without sentiment, self-critical in a politically aware manner rather than self-reflexive in a psycholiterary fashion: "I feel this is much more democratic and gets to the core of what the concerns of the entire circle [of participants] are" (p. 99). As with each of the texts, it references Houston-Jones's relationship with the body as a repository of actions being done to, and actions enacted upon.

It is, finally, an "I" clearly balanced in the context of its overall project, unapologetic, though not necessarily egocentric; through clear definition of parameters and possibilities arrived at through time, and a process aware of its own facture, Houston-Jones 'moves' through a manner of language that 'doubles' his style of physicality, listening carefully, having learned to ask questions without inserting a priori answers, using a method of abbreviated phrasing that, regardless, yields images of clarity and lucidity in texts that, in spite of their dark moments, remain determinedly humanistic.

AFTERIMAGE

The audience is seated in chairs that are scattered, at random, throughout the space. One of the performers leans over the right shoulder of one of the audience members and, gently rolling down, situates himself on the audience member's lap, requiring involvement, dispelling distance.

Kenneth King
Photo: Johan Elbers

autobiopathy

kenneth king

THE IDEA FOR THIS PIECE ACTUALLY occurred in 1972 while writing *Metagexis*. Instead of an autobiography, an *autobiopathy*—after Zen (and semiotics)—*the subject . . .* is supposed to disappear. Although I make notes and keep notebooks, I don't keep a "writer's diary" per se, hence this began as an open "ground" to try out, and write out, experiences and recollections in order to uncover their underlying formatory ideas. Since there is both a writer (1) and a dancer/choreographer (2) WHY NOT HAVE BOTH OF THEM TALK TO, AND INTERVIEW, ONE ANOTHER? . . .

. . .

2   What are you doing now?

1   Writing an *Autobiopathy*—what else!

2   An *AUTOBIOPATHY*? What's that?

1   Well, everyone writes an autobiography; but this is an *autobiopathy*.

2   Oh; perfect explanation. Is the *subject* the *disappearance* of the subject, again?

1   Uh-huh; and more than that, too . . .

2   *More*?

1   Yes, it's possible to write (ride) over oneself—we're just a collection of processes.

2   Oh, what an optimist! And another doubly reflexive entendre retort, too. . . . . The *technics* of disappearance?

1   Rather a writing out, over, and through experience—a survey of the transactional reapportionment of the subject's interprecessionary bioenergetic, perceptual, and cognitive processes.

2   Sounds like multimedia—not only the mixing of forms, but the mixing of processes, too. . . . The dancer, likewise, tries to dance over himself (recollecting Nietzsche).

1   Writing can place a subject between "brackets" or under virtual x-rays. The problem and challenge is to move the ego past itself (i.e. subjectivity per se) so the autooperation (or synchronous remodalization) of these bioenergetic and psychophysical processes prehend and apprehend themselves, mirror and reveal a larger, holistic "circuitry." And a note about the word *interprecessionary*—I discovered it in R. Buckminster Fuller's two-volume *Synergetics*; it's a very useful, systemic pivot.

2   In an analogous way dancing reflexes the elements, referencing a larger totality, too. Like swimming—while one's body is submerged in water the intraleveraged equilibria of the double, elemental reciprocity gives it suspension from gravity, and an orientation to another kinetic terrain: the watery. Similarly while dancing, one moves on fluidic ethers, electromagnetic currents and space circuits. "Dancing is writing in space"—and since *writing* is coextensive with all of language, so an autobiopathy can be the merging of self with a greater field and flow?

1   Yes, and insight into sentience revolves around the f(r)iction or illu-
     sion that we, as subjects, are separate—appearing, experiencing, then
     (eventually) . . . disappearing (which one can do from moment to
     moment, too—transposing the metaphor of passage). Each cell has
     sentiency, is vitally alive, participates in awareness, and like language,
     precedes and supersedes both perception and existence. We *think*
     that we learn, control, manipulate, or fix language; but language is
     culturally and genetically an independent (meta)entity—its combi-
     natory possibilities mean processes outrun ontology. Writing is not
     contained by a subject, but exceeds it; language too is a disembodied
     entity, and like a reservoir, potentiated and autogenic, i.e., beyond the
     parameters of any individuated intelligence. Language, no matter
     how accurately it mirrors mind, nature, or world, is also autorefer-
     ential; grammar, style and rhetoric create a self-referential, synchro-
     nistic, reflexive continuum. And the same with dance—the intensity
     and (implicit) immensity of movement transport one past (one's)
     identity, merging with a greater (sense of) being. The writer's fasci-
     nation lies, in part, with the autonomy of language that in turn
     informs and connects all processes and procedures of perception and
     experience. Art is a means of emptying or refocusing the subject's
     field. And, one doesn't know *what* one thinks until one asks oneself,
     or, doesn't really know it (perhaps) until one *interviews* oneself, or
     writes it out. The game thus involves a double reflexivity.

2   Or, of course, until it is danced out (or painted, sculpted, filmed, etc.),
     i.e., reflected through a virtual form. Likewise, there are some things
     that can be discovered only by dancing and that cannot be stated
     explicitly (or discursively), but that obliquely inform—at the margins
     and edges of b(B)eing (e.g. the mythic, spirit realms). Dancing is rid-
     ing through space—all space; space is not only three-dimensional.
     Dancing takes one beyond what one can know, or what knowing *is*;
     then it becomes enjoyable puzzling (through dialogue) what it is, or
     means, or what its correlates might be, in, with and *through* words.

1   Writing that concerns and engages me, though not always about
     dance, comes about because of dancing in the larger context of the

ontology of motion—movement of phenomena, dimensions, orders, contexts; and motion of words, thoughts, images, associations, worked over and through experience. And though I write at a word processor, it is not until we're home and dancing that I check and sound rhythms, *hear* text, edit or tighten syntactical structures, and launch the next probe. Perhaps not until the next century will the relevance of writing and dance (i.e. transmedia bridges across disciplines and bicameral potential) be realized; we've been making case studies . . . (Hence, the writer must dance and the dancer, write.)

Anyway, an *Autobiopathy*—how (one's) being is an intersection of ideas, issues, personas, beings. . . . ("All my pieces are ghost written," I've exclaimed hyperbolically on occasion.) To (double and) remove oneself so as to be a medium, to transmute the personal into art, activity, action. The *idea* of an autobiopathy requires a technic of writing to remove (absolve? make transparent?) the subject by exploring the foundations and underpinnings of ideas that (pre)figure the weaves of the self, and that inform its works, processes, activities and projects as transactive, semiolexic puzzles with unexpected configurations and metaconceptual matrices flexing perceptual, apperceptive and cognitive muscles.

And after all, "1" and "2" are just *processes,* separate but interrelated—and *intra*leveraged! (So what if they [we] share the same body, same house, etc.!) Ideas also "dance" interactively, intraconfigure systemically, become embodied and entrained, but are, nonetheless, always rooted in the mind of a specific identity (analogous to the way that any dance technique is always rooted in a specific *style,* there being no *pure* dance technique). The self becomes a site or scape as well as a foil for writing so the *personal* disappears; becomes reinscribed or *recircumscribed.* (And, unlike Bataille, writing on the impossibility of observing death while experiencing it, disappearance—Krishnamurti reminds us—can be a cosmic mode of meditation, and be virtually observable, transforming placements of the subject through metatheoria, and reflexivity, of hyperdimensional processes.) Metaphorically, an *autobiopsy,* like the successively generated pictures and macroscopically circular slices of a magnetic resonance imagery system (CAT scan), magnifies the inner structures and principles anterior to, and transcending, personal particulars—*auto*nomic imageries that trace the automimetic trajectories of the passages of flexions and impulses. A bioscopy of one's dances and texts; being an artist duly engages one in a series of virtual removes, and distances oneself personally and psychologically from being simply (or only) a subject—what's necessary are virtual *biopsies* of being's action and activities whose interactive contexts autosimulatively splice together and weave microviews and metaanalyse, compositing a larger field and overview. Hence, "X" is a kind of meta-, transpersonal and/or *transreferential,* subject—a reflexivized (meta)entity transmuting the impulses of ego and actions of self so that identity per se is recentered, de-, reconstructed, and transformed—by intrasynaptic processes, synoptic actions, renegotiable sights and hybrid languages that intersect, and interact with it. (Jung's clarification: the *self* orchestrates the parts and functions of body, ego, libido, etc.) This clarifies "deconstruction" to mean making transparent the processes and technics of analysis and perception (by microanalysis of word, unit and matrix), and the reflexions of those processes supraposed in assembling a larger whole.

2   That's what happens too when the body moves either very quickly or very slowly—other perceptually transpersonal processes transpire. What are your insights about the connection and differentiation of the *cellular* and the *genetic*?

1   Well, as a dancer you know that memory is not just neurological but extends through the cellularity of the body. At the same time, transformations in the whole organism become genetically entrained, as the "codes" underlying behavior and knowledge accrete and modify. Noam Chomsky's point about the transformation of language through generations—that linguistic capacity transfers automatically between generations—is actually a genetic statement. The child does not have to start at the beginning (e.g., with the rules of language); generations pass information incrementally, i.e., genetically. Is that another plié you're doing?

2   Yop. Then another and *another* after that. Thank goodness you're not a dancer, and spared this daily drudgery.

1   Ha! Try the umpteen zillion textual rewrites, and you'll change your mind.

2   Do I detect cynicism? Cynicism arises either from excess of experience or insight into the pervasive ethical deficiency of others.

1   Well, whether you know it or not, I get inspiration and ideas from you. You're my transmitter.

2   Really? How's that? You're the one that reads. I get all my ideas from you.

1   My point is that if I could write what are in your dances, I'd have more than book or treatise.

2   Well then, get busy! My point is that if I had your words for all the movements I do I'd be a millionaire.

1   Well, keep practicing, but don't get carried away. (Why I write texts— to be *done* with a dance! And so a reader might *feel* and *sense* them long after the fact.) Dialogue and dialectic—dialogizing exercises dialectic, i.e. multiple interpenetrating logics with transposable relation(s) . . . systems and systemics. Of course, this is a dialogue.

2   Well, they're (we're) not (not) separate and not not two.

1   You mean, we're not not the same person?

2   It seems to amount to the same thing—anyway, ontology in *extremis*.

1   You mean, of course we're not not the same person?

2   You mean, we're not not *being being* the same person again. But let's

save the lesson on Gertrude Stein, the ontologics and *ontotheletics* of grammar for later.

1   Exactly, *grammathics* again.

2   And riddles. And what could be more fascinating than ... grammato-logical riddles?!

1   Practically anything, including splitting hairs ... *or* one's identity.

1   Because our experiences of reading and using language double the ontological factor(s) ...

2   You mean you're the right brain in this bicameral brouhaha?

1   And you're the left hemisphere?! No, that's too literal—there are two parts and two intrapenetrating functions to perception, reading, and being an artist; one part observes and reflexes everything, (even the self that observes observation), and the concomitantly recombinatory, intraprecessionary processes of reflexion ...

. . .

1   Explain why you assign a complex and important role to improvisation as a basis for process dancemaking and choreography, and the development of dancers.

2   Improvisation begins as movement play and spontaneous exploration. It can also be highly structural, formal, and systemic. Though it is more a modern dance than balletic phenomenon, it can combine the principles and techniques of both. Improvisation reveals the grounds and roots of ritual, showing that dance goes even deeper than our bones, being bonded in our genes. Dance can distinguish, then fuse, the digital and genetic: this might be its artistic horizon and challenge in the next century.

Ritual and improvisation: when teaching dance composition one is continually astounded to see (even with beginning students) how deep the sources of ritualistic response are, like a kind of primal grammar, or genetic blueprint of automatic, prescient activity—and seemingly as integral to genes and cells as to muscle and brain—activating passages and pathways of coded mimetic transferences between bodies, extending bioenergetic fields to realms mythic and ancestral.

Because the moving, dancing body can systematically engage concurring, recurring and interprecessionary rhythms, patterns, structures and perceptual tracks (built up from concatenating chains of entrained flexions and iterative impulses) one can also learn to watch and see the semiotropic convergences of volleys of *signal* chains emerging into *signs* (usually first as gestures), and constellations of signs into structures. One sees symbolic transactions of movement phenomena in a dance continuum extending the kinetics and somatics of movement before and after form per se, as dreams break the bonds and bounds of reality and perception.

Improvisation shows *how the dance is a text*—it synergizes the elements of kinetic syntax and factors of composition (line, structure, form, exchange, spacing, rhythm, configuration, texture, import, etc.)—the volleying of shifting delays of signals and signs permutes and realigns the relays of contexts, transformed by the tiniest change of temporal, corporeal, muscular or spatial detail.

Even the making of a very formal and finished dance work can involve improvisational strategies at any stage of its creation. Improvisation is artistically prestructural, as images can be prescientific.[1] Movement itself is a motor and motive phenomenon; dance, an art.

Improvisation is more integral to (post)modern dance because its semiolexical deployments and structural principles are more fluid, less determined; experimentation is at its core. The ballet lexicon is basically a closed system, though any mode of movement can catalyze and open the parameters of any other given technique or style. Modern dance, basically an *open* system, is akin in its free-form modes to sketching, action painting, free verse poetry and automatic writing of the painter or writer. The liberation of forms from representation, literality, narrativity, and tradition was furthered by abstraction—abstract expressionist painting in the 1950s, happenings and performance art in the 1960s.

Improvisation loosens the boundaries between form(s) and content, styles and techniques, the set and unset, the continuous and discontinuous, the symmetrical and asymmetrical—creative antinomies, indeed— *and* between the known and unknown, contained and uncontained, bound and unbound, self and other, objective and subjective, motivation and intentionality—because movement connects through, across, over and around polarities, spaces, landscapes and dualities. Dance can be so spontaneous and vital (even with beginners) that it leaves the viewer bewildered—complex kinetic exchanges, sequences and passages need not be (pre)planned, organized, nor set. Thus improvisation recasts hierarchical stratifications; even virtuosic movement makes the watcher's eye sweep and scan the entire space and the configurative designs interactive with the other dancers, rather than holding a centralized (i.e. egoic) focus.

For observer and audience, improvisation generates different transactional modes of *seeing,* freed from expectation, presuppositions and assumptions—the simplest as well as an unexpected move or conjunction of gestures or patterned responses can surprise, connect, resonate or explode incredulously. Seeing, doing and making *can* be transactional and align modes by autoassemblage, where responses between bodies and dancers transpire faster it seems than the brain can think, presenting a new terrain and challenge. Improvisation reveals the spontaneous, organic dialectics of action dancemaking; it is the bridge between *process* and product.

Thus improvisation creates a site for multiply interactive processes. Where do our ideas about process originate? Undoubtedly from biology and physiology, and the fact that numerous autonomic (automatic) processes are intrapressional—digestion, sensation, breathing, circulation, respiration, reproduction, etc. The processes of improvisation project dynamically interactive, virtualized orders of imageries.

There is also a larger, more inclusive *systemic* and dialectical relationship between process(es) and system(s). The interaction of different processes compose the human biosystem. (As a choreographer I do not give dancers only specifically set, repeatable phrases, though we work toward that too, but rather pieces of phrases and steps that *they* have to recombine and work into the ongoing development of permutable structural schemas. These automatically build up volleys of steps and patternation options that can be reassembled and reordered to operate as rapid volleys of signs—as in-process indicators and recomposable clues for ways to assemble and order an ongoing dance's materials. This assembling is or makes a kinelexic grammar of dancemaking possibilities.) Language, too, moves between systems of categorical differentiations and schematic orders (typologies) of combinatory and assimilable spatial topologies. It is the idea of the matrix conjoining several compossible and simultaneous processes, modular components, body logics and digital rhythms, that allows for further systemic transformations, and that points to a new compositional concept.

Improvisation can reflect, *reflex* and make the totality of human experience(s) transparent, as well as its own factors (of experience or motivity—symbolic or structural, also able to mirror its own prestructuralities, rhythmic conflations, etc.). Improvisation can double back on itself to fold the accretions of the moving body into larger contexts. Improvisation shows that movement and dance can be self-reflexive of phenomena, mirroring essences. One need not start with 'a' structure and construct or compose 'a' dance—doing and making are reciprocally inseparable. This points to a kind of futuric ontology—dancing is *being being* seeing. Shiva is *before* the creation of the wor(l)d.

Some dancers breakthrough to genuine kinesthesia so spatial apperception creates fluent, fluid meshes between motivity, balance, form, alignments of corporeal and spatial isomorphisms, the harmonies of transspatiality ('geometry/typography') and the further ranges of transformative possibilities tempered by gradients of qualities plastic and/or emotive. Usually a dancer following rote choreography need never bother with decision making in performance (as Isadora Duncan did), nor with conceptual concerns (and concepts shift as our facts, feet, eyes and experiences change, realign, or, gather momentum); the entire (pr)axis of the (post)modernist matrix finds that its principles, lexical pivots, conceptual premises, structural and stylistic boundaries are indeed transactional—connecting forms, process, impulses, flexions and realms with other disciplines.

Improvisation constantly explores (modes of) *compossibility,* and moves between and through the first and last dance. There is comprehensive, *systemic* play generating a continuum of spontaneously synchronistic processes, and dance invites semiolexical transpositions (and in Merce Cunningham's instance, engineered, formally repeatable synchronistic processes, arrived at by chance procedures!). Coordinations of discontinuous, automatic motor sequences process raw passages of signals patterned into multiplex responses that weave the textural grains with the steady gain of momentum—that then congeal into concrete signs—reading indicators making transparent, eidetically identifiable traceries of line, design, structure, and gesture which coalesce symbolically as import, impact, resonance, and meaning, and reflexive, too, of natural forces, energy fields, and phenomena: rivers, eddies, whirlpools, waterfalls, vortexes, winds, currents, branchings, tributaries, etc.

The postmodern axis—or dance after Merce Cunningham—involves the (self-)reflexivity of movement principles and dance structures, breaking through to autonomous schematologies combining simultaneous logics and interactive body grammars. That these can be systemically open, observable, and coordinative *in and through the acts of* doing, deciding, making, dancing and seeing, is akin to the cognitive acumen necessary for creative problem solving, collectively experiential. (The idea that form as *performance* can be inclusive of interactive processes was polemically made explicit and extended by John Cage's pioneering, experimental music; in *Silence* he says why worry about structure—it's always there!)

There are motor-kinetic, tactile-somatic, and semiomimetic body grammars composing kinetic registers and kinelexic gradients—while reading, watching dance, film or television; even while talking, walking, thinking, and reading. The schematic complexes of "codes" that inform and navigate a dance's (or group's) course—and that coordinate the multiple dexterities of patterns, steps, and configurations—are both sub- and supraliminal. A dance can also incorporate written, spoken or projected texts with spoken or recorded voice, (electronic) music, projections and film/video to program simultaneous (and sometimes synaesthetic) processes. Even disjunctive and discontinuous processes can build up new senses of continuity and totality. Yet just *how* the intense enactments of impulses and responses, the concatenation of rhythms and qualities by one or more dancing bodies has analogues, axes and indexes grammatical, as well as grammatological, points to a further programmatic threshold utilizing multiple logics and pluralistic modes of intraprecessioning signal-sign assemblage. (Grammatological = orders of sign registers, schematologies of synchronous and asynchronous structurations. In the post-Cunningham, minimalist dance, simple everyday movement strategies structured in concrete, usually very repetitive and accumulative patterns, often with considerable systematic density, showed that themic and motific materials could be formally and contextually self-referential, and hence systemic within the parameters of its contained formal deployments.)

That *meaning* can be motor-mimetic involving the play of gradients throughout an energy continuum, that the eye can scan transliteral, kinelexic correlations and motoric-motive congruences, then polysemic structural schematologies involving multimedia principles and projections techniques, is rooted in interconceptual breakthroughs that eventuate in, and synthesize, new entrained orders, intrasensory ratios and logics and body grammars. Merce is the originary structuralist, and the diverse postmodern endeavors (and which really expanded the complexity of the highly refined, balletically oriented lexicon) prepared the ground for a grammatology of performative modalities and performance techniques.

These kinetically enhanced, programmatic extensions suggest other *digital* (and *digitated*) formats whose principles are reflexively and compositively analogical and that apprehend, then apperceive, further logicalities of electronic locomotion and passage through the transversed virtualities of space. This is proximally experienced in normal daily experience when trying to unscramble the jumbled, partial and puzzling recollections of dreams, assaying their fractured asymmetrical sequences, dislocated transitions, or disjunctive juxtapositions of elements and orders with actual referents and intimations of concrete meanings. Dancing, too, is like scrying with crystal ball or palimpsest.

· · ·

1   Before Richard Kostelanetz left for a vacation in 1991 he leant me the only copy of a manuscript for his forthcoming anthology of articles and criticism about Merce Cunningham, *Dancing in Space And Time.* It had just been readied for the publisher, and included my long *SPACE DANCE AND THE GALACTIC MATRIX: MERCE CUNNINGHAM, An Appreciation.* Presently, while proofing the galleys for publication by A Cappella Press, I (re)realized the expansive, all-encompassing endeavor necessary to develop a terminology suitable for an aesthetic overview to discuss his work—the pivot of modern and postmodern. (I worked on it during a three year period, from 1988 to 1991.) Just as there's a kind of transformative quantum jump moving a dance from rehearsal studio to stage, so too from typescript and manuscript to the printed page. This was the first piece I wrote on the word processor . . .

2   . . . And that I began *typing* on a temp job at Dean Witter Reynolds in the World Trade Center, luckily a do-nothing office job with plenty of "down" time! What readily amazed and became unexpectedly useful about writing on word processors were the time and labor-saving electronic options of cutting, moving, replicating, aligning, and altering

the text, which lets the writer readily learn editing techniques and spares retyping a piece in its entirety for each successive draft.

1   I started with that single, first paragraph. Like a kind of virtual replication it suggestively split into a second, and succeeding paragraphs. I resist writing from outlines and choose to organize my thoughts by assembling preliminary notes, fragments, possible sketches, and lists of issues. Sometimes the words come very quickly, requiring shorthand, or like a surgeon, very fast fingers. Writing is also cinematographic—contexts accrue without placement, and scenes are "shot" out of order; editing constructs continuity, focusing disparate logics and senses. Until actually beginning to write I'm not sure how contexts will configure their specific wording, structure or the grain of meanings, even, materializing in the process what I do *not* know, since hunches and the fleshing out of vague innuendo are part of any writer's compulsive fascination; one follows the *sense(s)* of a context or trails of an idea. Sketching a piece also begins to collect appropriate words and phrases, juggling and juxtaposing their possible syntaxing to (re)focus these emerging sense(s). The necessary modes of constant free and cross association intermix by throwing nets through the grids and depths of mental topologies thereby extending the parameters of word, sentence, and the structures of conception, letting eye and mind range and syncopate, and giving a buzz and sizzle to the act of writing. Writing is also like cooking—exotic spices and gourmet sauces—adjectives and adverbial clauses further temper the qualities and tensities, and elaborate the alignment of modes, eliciting the possible transconceptual gradients and giving an inkling of its emerging totality. Then a larger kind of editorial process works over weaves of contexts by pruning, rewriting, reordering, concision; lastly a fine tuning where a change of a single word or the repositioning of a phrase or sentence will complete a whole paragraph or piece.

Some days I write at length, other days only work on a single paragraph or sentence. Just as an oculist aligns multiple lenses, the writer layers a multiplicity of references, inferences, and networks of associability; contextuation generates and realigns the summating accretions of complexity or completion. There's also the problem of memory, history, and identity that further compounds the writer's (and language's) transformation(s)—hence Husserl's (*Ideas*) and Nietzsche's (*Ecce Homo*) reminders that truth is in the realm of fiction, albeit an elegant one. (Cognition is also a capacity to envisage, envision, *see.*) And it may be impossible to report anything objectively; writing transforms its contents and subject accordingly—the word relativizes experience and perception. Writing must be a *transmissivity,* not just documentation. Facts hurdle themselves.

And as I'm finishing the final first edit here, wondering about the readers it might reach I find this presciently evocative reminder in Georges Bataille's *Inner Experience*:

> I carry within me the concern for writing this book like a burden, I am *acted* upon. Even if nothing, absolutely, responded to the idea which I have of necessary interlocutors (or of necessary readers), the idea alone would act in me . . . the companion, the reader who acts upon me is discourse. Or yet still: the reader is discourse—it is he who speaks in me, who maintains in me the discourse intended for him. And no doubt, discourse is project, but even more than this it is that *other,* the reader . . .[2]

Writing is a continually challenging, probing process, and without doubt the word processor supplied the necessary next step. Between 1980 and 1983 I had written (that means entirely retyped numerous times) the long appreciations I was developing on Nietzsche, Susanne K. Langer, and Maria-Theresa Duncan. And of course one can *look* inside the old typewriters and see how they work mechanically, but the insides of electric typewriters and word processors are thin boards with microscopic transistors and multicolored, intricately coiled wiring. They're unfathomable, and their digital capacity instantly corrects spellings or moves one to a word or passage anywhere in a text with one or two keystrokes of a "Search" key, or copies, deletes, or replaces text (the software being virtually invisible). Word processors reinvoke, with a trenchant technological twist, the meaning of *wordsmith*.

. . .

1   How did you become interested in theater?

2   In kindergarten I had the lead as a farmer in a musical production and had to sing! It's a hazy memory and must have been dreadful! All I remember is the bustle of parents, the last-minute preparations, overdressing in two layers of clothes, a lot of straw, the final climb up the backstage stairs then having to perform while holding a little girl's hand on the very narrow edge of the stage apron in front of colored footlights, the lights obscuring almost everything else. A few years later I would have repetitive dreams that my bed was on that stage! Another curious memory (I must have been eleven or twelve) was going to see a magician (who was a friend of our family) perform a show of his tricks, and being envious of his assistant. Also my mother was glamorous and theatrical, though a horticulturist by profession.

As a kid I was intrigued by, and made, puppets, undoubtedly because of seeing early television shows, especially the unusually imaginative Bil and Cora Baird marionettes. (I was in second grade in 1950 when we got a TV, a "Phoenix," so I'm a card carrying member of the very first TV generation.) One puppet in particular, Spike, a stick puppet, exerted a special fascination—every day seated at a funky upright honky-tonk piano at the beginning of every show while playing and talking under and over the music, almost confidentially, in simpatico camaraderie to us kids at home—filling us in on the real scoop, the "dirt" or lowdown about what was about to happen, or what was really happening. He had a lean, gaunt face, like a steely tough with a cigarette dangling nonchalantly from the corner of his mouth, slits for eyes, heavy eyelids, and uncanny, mimetically mysterioso movements—jerky and quixotic like a pixilated phantom—droll, diabolical and scary (a spoof supposedly of the renowned jazz pianist Hoagie Carmichael). The way the (almost hidden) rods, connected at the wrists, controlled his taut, sharply angular verticality made the asymmetrical syncopation of his hands slightly disconnected, unreal and suspect, enhancing his spooky but captivating, endearing anonymity; there was something about his identity that was, or had to be, concealed. (His movements suggested something that could only be surmised, since I probably had no real idea of mystery at that age.) Spike gave me the chills, intriguingly quickening the prescient sense of mystery and play; he inspired a secret allure, allied with the forbidden and unknown.

Later, my parents had a puppet stage built for me as a Christmas gift that could be used for both marionettes and hand puppets, with a red velvet draw curtain, stage apron and little footlights. I made my own puppets—out of almost anything, constructed and performed homemade shows for my friends and baby brother, Grant, in the cellar playroom (real underground). One was an exaggerated Tallulah puppet, with some Auntie Mame mixed in—imperious, unreal, and with an archly ridiculous voice. Looking back I realize there's another virtual ontology to the animation of puppets that suddenly transforms them from static and sometimes simple objects into *beings* that seem to have a life of their own—a kinetic semblance that is a "virtual illusion"—and *more*! The disembodied kinetics of puppetry—being moved *from beyond* the confines of the body, the transformation of inspired play and shifting textures of imaginary voices—impacted on my early dancing. I guess I secretly wanted to be the puppets and still be able to pull the strings!

We would go to our grandparents' large, old house for Thanksgivings (over 150 years old, with over twenty rooms, built with wooden pegs instead of nails); their third-floor attic, hermetic and remote, had drawers, closets and trunks full of vintage clothing and turn-of-the-century costumes. My cousins and I loved going through the outdated garments and gear and dressing up in outlandish getups. After Thanksgiving dinner we would try to do impromptu shows, but the grown-ups always passed out—sounds *avant-garde*, right?! It was in their attic that I also found a variety of fabrics for my puppets as well as when I first sensed invisible presences.

Another early TV show that had a big impact on my imagination was *Beat The Clock*. It was sponsored by Sylvania, with a large lit-up clock used to measure the allotted time (in seconds) for each stunt. Married couples were the contestants, and the handsome, smooth, and charming emcee (Bud Collier) had a fetching, pretty blond assistant, Roxanne—sort of a 1950s X-rated "fantasy gal" in a snug black, lowcut frock or cocktail dress who sparked the proper *innuendo*. There were basically two kinds of *fraught*, unreal stunts for the contestants attempting to win tempting prizes (appliances, vacations, etc.). The first type featured improbable and near impossible riggings with props, stands, containers with fluids, and relay races. Each couple as a team was more often placed in baleful opposition to one another; the wife had to try coordinating some difficult tasks with gear like fishing poles, tilted platforms, precariously balanced cups or containers, whipped cream (their favorite) to avert an accident with the husband getting squirted, mauled, pummeled, whip-creamed or clobbered (not so subtle revenge). Roxanne was always there to clean up the embarrassed or humiliated husband, emerging ruefully from his plastic, protective suit, while the audience howled. People replicated the scenarios at parties. The other task involved *language*—a curtain opening rapidly to reveal a blackboard with a famous scrambled aphorism or saying. Each word had magnetic holds so they could be quickly repositioned. The time element, and the large, loud ticking clock (twenty seconds, usually) were anxiety- and suspense-provoking. This is what a writer is *always* doing to syntax—repositioning every word to gainsay the sentence. The show's improbable stunts, paraphernalia and bizarre accoutrements were an obvious, humorous setup, and undoubtedly the irrational, motley collection of improbable props and gear influenced my early dances. I still trace my fascination with sex perversions to this show—it was like a pop Krafft-Ebbing turned into not-so-sublimated *charades* (later I found an old, yellowed edition hidden in my parents closet!). TV *is* perverse.

notes

1   Cf. Susanne K. Langer, see esp. the Introduction and Part I of *Mind: An Essay on Human Feeling*, Volume I (Baltimore: Johns Hopkins University Press, 1968).

2   Bataille, Georges, *Inner Experience*, translated by Leslie Anne Boldt, (Albany, NY: State University of New York Press, 1988), 60 (emphasis Bataille's).

commentary

IMAGE

A cone of sand is created by a random action of wind over a vast stretch of beach. A man, no, a woman, no, a man, no, a woman, no, a sentient being of indeterminate grammar sees the cone, walks around it, decides it is a false nose, the beach is wearing a false nose, one foot high. The cone's observer hears the sound of waves. Leaning back to scrutinize the cone, the observer/listener spots a rubber ball. Picking it up, the ball is placed between the observer/listener/biter's teeth as the name of every childhood street is repeated backwards, naming the waves.

REFLECTION

In naming, we establish ourselves as a species of language makers, or as Kenneth King postulates, language takers: "Each cell has sentiency, is vitally alive, participates in awareness, and *like language, precedes and supersedes both perception and existence*" (italics mine); everything in this cosmology is eternal, pre-existent, and knowing.

King's passionate strategy is often paradoxical.[1] An early exponent of what came to be called postmodernism, much of King's "Autobiopathy" reads as seventeenth century Western metaphysics laced with Zen, though his vocabulary—with embellishments— rests in the still-European-influenced, language-philosophy twentieth; century markers are arbitrary, and rests is not an appropriate verb to describe King's writing. The first sections of the excerpts of "Autobiopathy" included in *Footnotes*, pages 108 through 121, speed in the way of an electric current, a structurally propulsive effect achieved by the length of compound, often italicized neologisms, which guide the eye rightward. Long complex sentences, with liberal comma-usage, contribute to the sense of flowing speed, as of something scrolling, moving. The subject in these sections is encoded, enshrouded, an energized but blurred "us" or "we," in a primarily present tense. The flow could be read as an analogue for the experience of dancing or watching dance. The text maintains its pace once the reader decides not to let the arcane terminology compel her own ego to slow it down, try to control it, decipher all the newly formed words and densely enunciated concepts but to read somewhere between her own ability to apprehend its meaning and the writer's desired effect as she perceives it, an attempt to convey the experience of experiencing, in written language. The eyes read, the eyes "listen."

King continues the evidently self-reflexive interview he has conducted throughout between a dancer-self and a writer-self, but in the last sections included here, pages 122 through 124, the vocabulary is familiar, the tempo normalized. It is closer to the technique used to interview well-known personages in the form of popular stars, in the formulation of the final question and the structure of its response. The persona is chatty, charming, a seemingly accessible "I," the split self on the way to being mended, if only by determination, the "I" of snapshots in the family photo album, the "I" of memory's reportage, the "I was."

King defines the word autobiopathy tautologically. The word commands our attention. The change of the final syllable from *graphy* to *pathy* is a quiet explosion. The word breaks down as self/life/suffering. It is an interesting decision for King to have made, whether by casting about, consciously looking, or through a more unconscious intuition; the reader is not privy to the origin of the choice, and King does not divulge it, may not know the answer himself. Suffering, in the Buddhist sense, is brought about by our desires, our attempts to fix firmly, grasp, hold onto instead of acknowledging the changing nature of ourselves and all that surrounds us.

After the title, King begins by tacitly posing a solution to a problem that has tested physics, diplomacy, and party-hosting the world over. He privileges the number "2" by giving it first place, therefore, by implication and habit-of-thought, having "1" (the writer) and "2" (the dancer) conceptually occupy the same place simultaneously, a scientific and logical conundrum that King dispatches with finesse and devil-may-care gusto. Thus the dancer, usually silent, is the first voice we hear.

King's persona is enthusiastic, confident, demanding; his self-reflexive word-jamming can be intimidating, off-putting, dismissed as jabberwocky. This is to misconstrue, I think, the consciously playful aspects of King's project, its intended seriousness and sense of purpose or mission. This experience exists as a process of examination of the ways in which dance and movement count as something important, the ways in which spoken or written words and fully actualized dance movements enunciate ideas of self, what contradistinct vocabularies convey, how they interact and communicate to and with each other as read, seen. *Pace* verbal or written language, and for all his word fervor, King does not capitulate to word language as superior, but views it as a tool and, in Kingly fashion, would gladly dub a spoon a hammer, as long as it can be used to hit a nail, and why not? In turning the semiotic up a notch, he displays a fearlessness and audacity that enlists it in the service of art-making, putting dance on equal footing with philosophy: "[T]here are some things that can only be discovered by dancing and that cannot be stated explicitly (or discursively). . . " (p. 109). It challenges those who would claim that their language investigations encompass or subsume all. It is a unique position King occupies: a dancer has not only read the literature, but allowed it to substantially infiltrate, penetrate, become part of his praxis; he has become a spokes-dance-person. How many philosophers, current or post, regardless of how much dance analogy or imagery they use, could address, firsthand, the following: "Dancing also tells us what cannot (yet) be put into words, connecting mind and body."

AFTERIMAGE

A tall thin figure on half-point, arms raised overhead, spins through a large, dark space, holding aloft two small lights, as though a conduit, summoning the energy of the spheres.

notes

1   A note about the use of the word strategy when applied to art-making. It obtained *vernacular* agency in the 1980s in reference to the visual arts. Its relationship to war is not only connotative, but explicit. Where it might refer to a slice-of-life scenario between art-makers and those who would see art destroyed, it seems appropriate. Where it denies a process it denies intuition, is airless, dominating, dismissive of rough edges and doubt. It is, in short, a macho proposition. Thus, used in *Footnotes,* its use is also disclaimed, or qualified. My own paradox.

Yvonne Meier
Photo: Lina Pallotta

the shining

yvonne meier

THE SHINING, A DANCE WORK, DEALS with the world of fearful anxiety and thrill; it reveals the double bind of those emotions, a postmodern fusion. It speaks of experiences at once sought and avoided—how do we hide from fear, play with thrills and terrors, how do those emotions excluded from consciousness play with us?

The tense draw of childhood memory finds its way through a labyrinth; the pleasant shock of a hand appearing in the dark, the titillation of a thriller, the game with the macho Western hero who is longing with fear to move the play forward while threatening images—images of horror, brutality, gang fights and war—dominate the stage.

Common rituals of movement are examined for elements of dance: rough-housing between children, fights during soccer games, fits of anger and hysteria. The movements develop into a speedy crescendo of violent impacts and sudden jerks: driven by escalating energy and fear, we run from cruel pursuers, trapped in a nightmare prison without light, without exit, caught in a claustrophobic corner.

The Shining works with our fears and the tensions they create in our bodies, tensions invisible under most circumstances, unspoken fears. The piece grasps this potential and allows the audience to experience classic catharsis. *The Shining* is a mirrored dramatization of our interior life. The illusion is that of being inside the mind of a dreamer.

the installation

The concept of the installation calls for a room filled to the ceiling with approximately 350 cardboard refrigerator boxes. The cartons function as a laboratory, as a labyrinth of hidden spaces and high sculptures. Secret passageways allow for the performers to appear in ways inexplicable to the audience (see fig. 1). This contributes to the tension of insecurity and surprise conducive to the piece's subject matter.

Completely filling the room with objects changes the sense of space. Through a tiny entrance the audience slips into a "subterranean city." Flashlights in the hands of the performers provide the only source of light. As a result, the audience is, at times, literally left in the dark, disoriented. Using their hands to guide them, the spectators begin to find their way through tight tunnels, knowing neither where they are going nor what is going on. Instead of a purely visual experience the performance turns into a kinesthetic one.

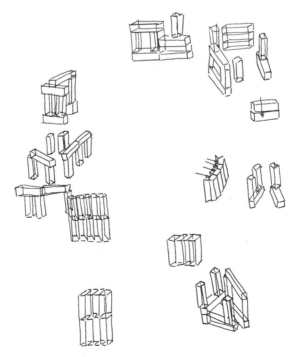

Fig. 1

three radical ideas
about audience

The installation allows the traditional concept of the space-performer-audi-
ence relationship to dissolve in a way that not only involves the spectators, but
turns them into the piece itself.

1. Performing space and audience space are identical:
    —The audience is situated within the space.
    —Every spectator is introduced into the space without his/her
    knowledge of what is going to happen.
    —The spectators on several occasions move independently through
    the space without any kind of directives or requests.

2. The audience interacts with the performers:
    —The dancers/performers initiate contact directly with the specta-
    tors, and involve them in the overall action and specific movements.
    For example, members of the audience undergo a police "pat down"
    body check, or they are carried through the labyrinth. They are
    twirled, rolled around, surprised by dancers and danced *to* and *at*.

3. Simultaneity of action:
    —Several scenes take place at the same time in different rooms,while
    the audience is left mostly to search for and discover secrets.

At different times the audience is placed at specific locations. The necessity for
this will reveal itself to the spectator by the following occasionally wild or even
dangerous scenes.

Constantly alternating between complete freedom to walk through
unknown rooms, sudden entrapment or being pushed into a corner, the resulting feeling of barely having escaped rattles the audience, keeps it under high tension and attention.

the course of the piece

INTRODUCTION INTO THE LABYRINTH

Each member of the audience is led separately to the entrance of the spiral-shaped labyrinth in intervals of three minutes (fig. 2).

The room is completely dark. The only light sources are the flashlights each performer carries. Figures appear and disappear. Lights flash briefly.

Boxes are moved, and a pair of eyes staring from a box surprise the spectators.

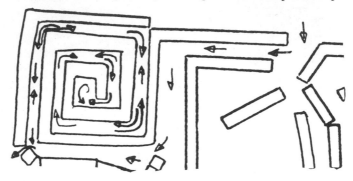

Fig. 2

FUNNY ROOM

Once spectators have made their way through the spiral they are led to a point where another performer picks each one up and pulls them into the Funny Room (fig. 3).

Giving into the relatively safe feeling of being guided, the spectator follows the leader (Führer), who plays with the structure of the Funny Room by suddenly appearing and disappearing; a chase begins, developing according to the reactions of the audience member.

Fig. 3

FRENCH MUSEUM

The audience is led into the French Museum — where they are left, more or less,
to themselves (fig. 4).

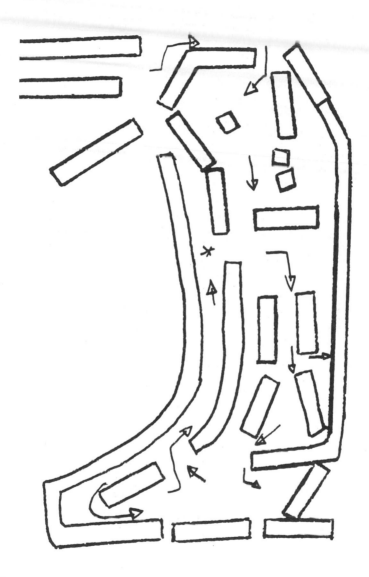

Fig. 4

AQUARIUM

A mummy-like twitching dance is performed inside an aquarium-like box construction (lit by a dim flashlight—fig. 5).

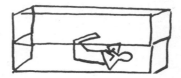

Fig. 5

DANCING BOXES

Two boxes are standing on top of a third. The two boxes are being manipulated by a person inside box three —the boxes seem to move by themselves (fig. 6).

Secret pathways are constructed through boxes laid down; dancers can disappear and appear in and out of them. At the points marked * the audience members get picked up and led to the next section of the piece.

Fig. 6

THE JOURNEY

At the same time as segments from the film music of *The Sisters* by Bernard Herrmann are being played, one also hears a piece by Elliot Sharp. Each member of the audience is taken by the hand and led by the performer into the larger rooms. The ensuing interaction begins with fixed "concerted movement." For example, the 'spectator' is placed in a corner and hands "wash" the entire body. Or he is put on a chair as part of an installation, instructed to move his upper body up and down. Sometimes the spectator is abandoned to be picked up and led by another performer.

Interaction between audience and performer develops based on the reaction of the audience to some manipulations: rolling them on the floor, being lifted, etc. Over time, a duet may happen with an audience member.

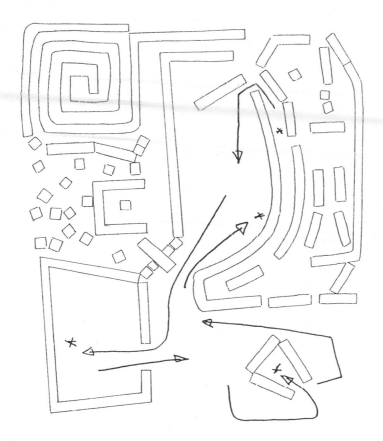

Fig. 7

In-between Sections

PART I

While part of the audience is led through the journey, a duet emerges as dancers hold their own flashlights. Through movement of their flashlights, sections of themselves and their partners are lit as they move (fig. 8).

A second duet emerges as performer **A** folds up Performer **B**. **B** will explode out of the folding, and so on. Music "1" is overlapped with a new music piece leading into:

PART II

A person on top of a ladder swings a lamp, resembling a lighthouse.

Fig. 8

PART III

COWBOY/WESTERN SCENE

Music. Performer A plays with the rhythm, pretending to ride on a horse as her feet propel her horse forward. Two flashlights on A's side become two guns as their light beams point to Performer B, who is shown doing a dance as if being shot repeatedly. B stands against the opposite wall (fig. 9).

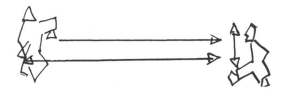

Fig. 9

The beam of the flashlight, as **A** turns slowly, is seen as a sunset over the box city (fig. 10).

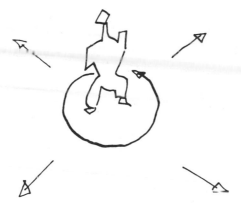

Fig. 10

DREAM SEQUENCE

This sequence is composed of the following dreamlike elements as they appear. They are either simultaneous or overlapping, and seem to come out of nowhere and vanish into the darkness (fig. 11).

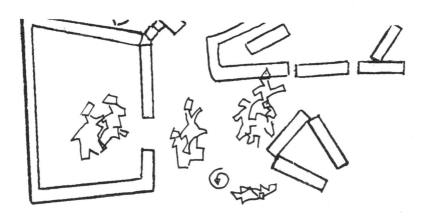

Fig. 11

MANIPULATED THROW DANCE (INSIDE BOX ROOM)

A is pulling **B** up by his head and then begins to throw **B**'s arms around. **B** remains passive most of the time except every now and then, when he makes attempts to change directions of the throw.

ROLLING AGAINST THE WALL

Seemingly pointless and disparate. Towers of people appear in different places in the half-dark.

STYLISTIC SLOW-MOTION SCENE (DUET)

A lifts **B**'s feet while moving through, under, and away from them.

SHADOW SCENE (THRILLER)

One performer turns slowly, lighting her own hand with a flashlight that casts an enormous shadow onto the box city. Quiet murder scenes are in progress as two other performers join in the turning. A shadow play stirs on the wall (fig. 12).

Fig. 12

ALLEGRO

This fast and explosive dance travels in and out of three different spaces, forcing the audience into a corner for its own protection. The dance score is dangerous, and the set lit simply by a lone blinking flashlight in motion. Definition of the room dissolves. Finally, the audience is drawn into the box room—backed up against its wall—as performers build a pile of bodies in the center of the room (fig. 13).

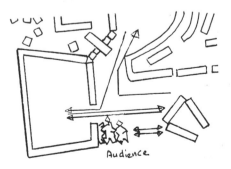

Fig. 13

In the "gate" behind the pile, a murder scene plays repeatedly.

PREVENTED DANCE

The audience remains against the back of the box room as a violent duet develops. **A** is presenting a mad, "disco flying dance" layered behind various dancers who appear and disappear, creating the effect of a slide projector (fig. 14).

Fig. 14

THREATENING SILHOUETTE DANCE

Lit only by a light source from behind, a dancer performs a threatening dance inches away from the audience. The audience is unable to make out the face of the performer. Only the silhouette is visible. The dancer himself cannot judge distances, which highlights a sense of danger. Other performers begin to lead each audience member around the silhouette and into the open box room (fig. 15).

Fig. 15

Each audience member gets stuffed into his or her own box and is instructed not to move (fig. 16).

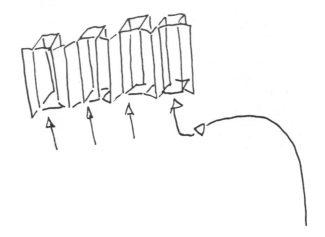

Fig. 16

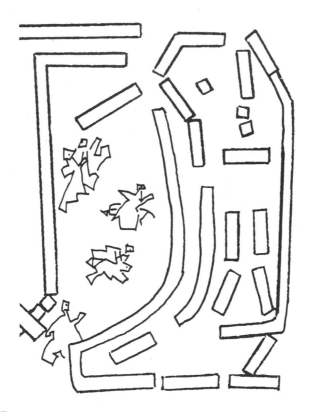

Fig. 17

HIGHPOINT

Themes of the piece are being picked up and put together into a seemingly chaotic nightmare-like scenario. Towers of boxes crash down. Boxes are catapulted over the heads of the audience. A general collapse of order is displayed. Sparse and flickering lights enhance the apocalypse (fig. 17).

LAST PART

Again, the audience is split up into groups and led back into the dimly lit maze. At this point, the interaction/exchange of the audience and dancers occurs to where the audience feels as though they've become part of the piece.

The dancers begin to pull audience members out of the space. The performance ends when the final member of the audience is removed.

END

aspects of the work

Classical dance is isolated from material and tends to depend primarily on abstract physical expression. My work brings together materiality and body language; my pieces are characterized by the strongly visual as well as an intense relationship to the stage-set and props.

Over the years I have developed the following principles which keep appearing in my work in various forms:

1) Transformation of the entire stage-set into a prop, an object which becomes a partner in motion; the reverse also holds true: props turn into the stage set.

2) I usually construct my own props and stage-sets. I am particularly interested in "estranging" objects by enlargement, both in scale as well as in numbers (multiplication).

The cardboard labyrinth, for example, creates a response. The crammed spaces, the frighteningly small loopholes, and the box towers threatening to tumble down, put dancers and spectators into a state of alarm, a state of "What if . . . ?" The stage material becomes a partner in the movement, one that influences us, puts us into trance, changes our perception of reality.

In my recent pieces I have used mundane objects as props: kitchen utensils, plates, and pans, and heads of lettuce. I work, increasingly, with dimensions of size—enlargement in scale as well as in number. The familiar object of a cardboard box becomes building material, building blocks to an expanding, exaggerated nightmare fantasy.

POMMES FRITZ (1991)

A gigantic shelf construction—filled with 1,000 plates—created the backdrop (fig. 18). The construction was made to be destroyed. As the shelves collapsed, all 1,000 plates fell to the floor.

Yvonne Meier, left
Jennifer Monson, right
Photo: Dona Ann McAdams

Fig. 18

Especially in my solo performances, I have developed "a principle of parallel circuits."

CIRCUIT 1. Relationship of the dance-parts to one another.
CIRCUIT 2. My relationship to the objects.
CIRCUIT 3. The relationship of the objects to me.
CIRCUIT 4. The relationship of the objects to one another.

The objects chosen for my solo performances are personal. The performances are extremely active, in the course of which the stage is completely changed. The actions/objects are specific to each piece.

choreographic topics

For the last thirteen years I have examined the development of choreographies as well as the development of concepts of movements. Besides traditional choreographic technique my work often requires the development of new concepts (rules) and conditions in order to achieve maximum results.

Examples:

—Explosive duets

—Unexpected involvement of gravity (i.e., the floor)

—Development of the maximum risk in movement and series of movements: by exploring rules or scores I try to expand a dancer's personal language of movement (*by also applying restrictions of rules*).

The following analogy seems to describe this adequately: the dance of concepts is like walking through a hallway with many doors, each of which is the entrance to a new part of the house.

This concept turns the preparations for the performances into a process of learning, implying a change of consciousness on the part of the dancers. My goal is to transfer this effect, during performance, to the audience. An example is the change of consciousness via exhaustion.

At least half of my rehearsal time is dedicated to this aspect of the work and has resulted in the following examples:

—Radical change of pace in the middle of a movement.

—Exploration and use of various "percentage" tension in different parts of the body.

—Following secondary impulses.

—Waiting for, or initiation of, a "natural" stop.

—Use of weight in different parts of the body.

—Legs dance in a pulse, arms make gestures.

—Blocking the effect of the flow of movement in various parts of the body.

—Various approaches to movement: attacking, sensuous, nonchalant, and so on.

—Opposition of qualities, like raw and ornamental.

commentary

IMAGE

Outside, under a sky releasing rain as if from a leaky cistern, a rubber ball caroms across a latticed floor, surface of glass. The floor is only slightly suspended above a pool of one hundred snapping turtles, outfitted with castanets. When we look closer, the ball is actually a woman, blindfolded, curled up and springing, rolling, bouncing, rebounding, managing to hit the corners of the lattice. It is all taking place in pitch dark, lit only by a single bulb's stark illumination.

REFLECTION

Yvonne Meier's "The Shining," a conventionally descriptive text supplemented by complementary renderings, is used to illustrate an unconventional choreographic project. It rightly conveys the impression of one whose first language remains the body, a universal condition often overlooked, taken for granted. Prior to verbal skills, we find ourselves living inside the body, recipients of the effects of encoded messages in our genes, the experience of the womb, and later, the profusion of information we receive from others, contradicting or confirming what we perceive when we look in the mirror. As contradictions outdistance conflations, we become further fragmented.

Meier's first spoken language is Swiss German, the language in which the text for "The Shining" was originally written. It was written as a grant proposal, a form of writing valid in the the current project because relevant in its specificity as a reference to the economics of dance.

In conversation with Meier, she explained that her earliest dance experience in Zurich was classical ballet, which she began studying as a child. Meier was convinced of the rightness of dance as a form in which to express herself, but her small, compact stature did not qualify her to be taken seriously in a classical form with restricted, stringent codes, it created a breach between her experience and the response of others. She next tried jazz, with much the same result. Eventually encountering modern dance, she came to the United States to study at Merce Cunningham's studio; this, too, proved unsatisfactory as Meier, short and standing in the back of the room, felt she was still not present to others in a manner that matched her intention or desire, her wish to perform.

The foregoing is also illustration, but germane in light of Meier's project; she deals with the language and text of the body almost exclusively, with spoken language used

arah Skaggs
oto: Mary Gearhart

sparingly, when at all, as no-frills improvisation. Deciding to remain in New York City, Meier began studying release work with Joan Skinner and, elsewhere, participating in contact improvisation workshops. In either, the 'organ of speech' is used as a practical tool to communicate its initial intention—as if, when walking into a house, someone said, "Hang your coat there"—but spoken language is comparatively relegated, and the emphasis placed on the experience of the body. She has since taken these two languages—the former *internalized,* singular to one's own deep-body experience, similar to thought, the latter *externalized,* done in concert with others, similar to speech—and utilized them in a manner analogous to written or spoken language experiments, breaching their boundaries, moving among the found "texts" of both and pushing them, and herself, into new territory.

Both release work and contact improvisation replace the emphasis on the way one looks with the way one experiences, as if contrasting diction or rules of grammar with the process of thought. The forms themselves had a radical influence on postmodern performance. Meier's experience with release work led to a paradox: while signaling an exposure of the self to itself that had not existed previously, and with body *type* no longer an issue, Meier perceived that her body could be used as another object, a prop. This reification led Meier to an investigation of what might be seen as the human prop as protagonist, the nonhuman as antagonist. The idea that people are not *things,* became translated into things having an equal presence that can inform their human counterparts as further collaborators in the project, focusing attention on that which shares the stage, further sensitizing the viewer to objects in the world.

By multiplying the number of a given object—cardboard boxes, plates, heads of lettuce—Meier gives them presence, body, voice. Reification of the performer also serves to displace the "I" in this dialogue. These are simultaneous conversations: the self with the self, the self with others, self and other with inanimate objects. In the live event, *The Shining,* these concerns reach their apogee. The performers interact with self, other, prop, as do the audience/participants. In this and other work, when Meier *does* insert speech it is as a practical means of instruction to the participants, whether rehearsed performers or, as in *The Shining,* both performers and audience members.

In the project, Meier enacts a form of playful terrorism, at times benign, at others more threatening—one which, without the physical or literal voice of interrogation, speaks to internal mechanisms of fear and intimidation, to the questions we articulate internally concerning what we might do in situations of actual physical intimidation; it relies on this internal voice for its meaning, raising questions of the audience/participant's ability or willingness to trust, to relinquish control. One's own text, is engaged, becomes acutely attuned to the unexpected, as the body is propelled through darkness, by barely seen others. This dialogue with dislocation was unsettling enough for some that, in the case of one potential funder, there was a refusal to participate when confronted by the prospect of the initial step, or blunder, into a dark, unrecognizable, space. In another case, funding for subsequent performances was denied on the grounds that participation in *The Shining* could perpetuate irreversible mental damage.

The number of audience members is intentionally limited in contrast to the profusion of boxes—some standing tall, others requiring the participant to kneel down and crawl in. It creates an experience of disorientation: darkness mitigated only by flashlights (the beams of which are often swung around, creating further disorientation), whispers, spoken instructions, physical handling of audience members by rehearsed performers. It creates an increased awareness of the moment and one's own vulnerability to ancient fears and the desire for safety, while wanting to experience the fear, to see it as play. The darkness, the labyrinth, the inescapable voices of the performer/instructors, translate into a metaphor for the psyche. I address this as a participant/audience member. It encourages, as Meier's states, " . . . the audience to experience classic catharis" (p. 130).

The physical risks Meier takes, and the methodology she employs in her work, allow for multiple readings, as when she transposes or rearranges several previous pieces—and their original props—into one new piece, and in this juxtaposition, opens the text to new possibilities of interpretation. Meier is a virtuosic improviser, a mode that is close to the function spoken language performs in everyday conversation. In the specifically choreographed work, there is an edge of flamboyance, contoured by her deadpan demeanor and her clownlike costuming which, when not a further extension of her props, may be read in much the way we read silent film clowns such as Charlie Chaplin or Buster Keaton. When 1,000 plates on shelves are bought crashing to the ground, we can read this as absurdity in numbers, as frustration at our own sinkful of dishes waiting for us at home, as the noise and smoke after an explosion.

The drawings that are included with "The Shining" are a further indication of Meier's mistrust of written (or spoken) language as a means to articulate her ideas, even in her

native language. As rehearsal tool, or when Meier leads workshops, she 'composes' scores for the participants to work with, or from; it is of note that these scores, though initially communicated in words, take their terminology—that is, the word, *score*—from the nonverbal world of music. I have circumvented Meier's position, supplanted it, invaded it. Her written description of *The Shining* is marked by necessity; it resists articulating the sub rosa speech that swims inside a silent, but constant text, propelled by the body/mind, even as it stills the speaker's tongue, the writer's hand.

AFTERIMAGE

A woman, as if catapulted, hurls herself through space, lands, throws her head and upper body toward the floor while suspended on one leg, the other leg flung up sharply behind her, pulling her off balance; she puts herself in a defiant, precarious state of pleasure.

paradise
remixed

sarah skaggs

DANCE, IN MANY PARTS OF THE WORLD, is used as a cultural adhesive, providing a medium through which people can find a mate, celebrate a specific occasion, or prepare for competition or war. I always wondered how certain civilizations went from participating in a dance event to consuming "an evening of dance." My choreography is an attempt to rearrange and shift the way people receive culture in the United States, to change the way we perceive and participate in dance. I want to address that point in our history where a separation occurred between those who *do* and those who *watch*. I have spent the last six years synthesizing many influences, inspirations and ideas to try and establish a new (by reestablishing an old) format in which people experience dance. This idea involves creating dance events (as opposed to concerts) in non-proscenium venues: gymnasiums, clubs, ballrooms, parks, or any place people congregate or associate with socializing.

bali

A trip I took to Bali in 1992 was an epiphany. For the first time, I saw a culture intact, not compartmentalized. There was very little separation between every-day life, religious or spiritual life, and all forms of art, including dance; the secular and sacred were never far apart.

In Bali, I traveled on my bike to villages where I was the only non-Asian. I was dressed in the sarong and taken into temples where I witnessed an incredible mixture of "hanging out," milling around, and trance dance. The shrines were filled with offerings such as oranges, lemons, palm leaves, paper cups, fabrics, and flowers—items from everyday life, not golden goblets. Life centered around the temple complex. It was a bustling mixture of commerce (for example, stalls with bras, sandals, and underwear for sale), socializing, eating, and gambling on the cockfights. The mixture of activity boggled the mind. There, dance is a part of everyday life. It functions as a model for social order, illustrating the people's complex cosmology and insuring—through the stories in their dances—a balanced society of cooperation, not competition.

The trip reaffirmed many ideas I had had for a long time concerning dance events that are ritualistic in nature and, ultimately, communal. I needed to figure out how to translate these ideas into my own culture. I began to look for references in American culture where people have come together to socialize (from the Latin *socius,* meaning companion): sock hops, small town Saturday night dances, and block parties. Working with me on this project was Mary Gearhart (lighting designer/photographer/videographer) with whom I have been collaborating for twenty years. We began to look for spaces in which to construct the project that I had begun to formulate (originally called *Higher Ground*, it subsequently became known as *The Miracle on Mulberry Street*).

the miracle

When I returned from Bali, I searched New York City for the right space to build *Higher Ground*. I started by running around to the most obvious places: dance clubs such as the Limelight, Webster Hall, and Roseland. Then Mary—not only my collaborator and friend but a fellow longtime resident of Little Italy — suggested the gymnasium of the old St. Patrick's Cathedral on Mulberry Street. It was a terrific idea, one that coincided with my need to connect with the neighborhood I live in.

Little Italy, unlike many other neighborhoods in the city, is clearly defined on all four sides: going north-south, from Houston to Grand Streets, and east-west, from Bowery to Lafayette Streets, it almost replicates a small town. In small towns in America, everyone has a function; that makes them similar to Bali, where the code of cooperation is determined by their farming culture. Our neighborhood, too, reflects a kind of cooperative spirit initiated by the Irish, Italian, and Hispanic people who settled here, while still maintaining the rhythms of their respective cultures. As an artist, dancer, and newcomer to the neighborhood, I was known as "the ballerina," an attempt to define my profession. My neighbors knew I danced but had never seen me do it. I knew they would never come to see my shows at Dance Theater Workshop, the Danspace Project at St. Mark's Church, or P.S. 122,—all dance or theater venues in downtown Manhattan. The audiences who come to performances at these spaces are "dance audiences" — those who are already informed, and follow dance. I was always concerned that more of the general public (however we define it) didn't come to witness the wonderful work of my comrades in these spaces. How could I change this situation and create something in my own neighborhood that would draw a traditional dance audience, as well as the local residents?

For a long time, I have been interested in the concept of a neighborhood and a community that occurs naturally, as opposed to artificially constructed or "gated" communities. I believe the development of the suburb has destroyed the communal concept of neighborhoods and consequently has had a profound effect on Americans' relationship to art. Small towns had halls for Saturday night dances, town political meetings, and small theater productions, in which everyone played a part. People played the piano, sang songs, and read books. The word "community"—common-unity—had true meaning. Suburbs were often the opposite; they meant privacy, the idea of getting away from your neighbors.

This has led me to read up on various architects and city planners who are working to rebuild the concept of a neighborhood in an effort to counter suburban sprawl and the alienation that comes with it. Visionary architects Andres Duany and Elizabeth Plater-Zyberk look to older models, such as the village, to create a new urbanism in contrast to the suburb, whose structure was built entirely around the automobile. A "village" is defined as a cluster of homes around a central place that is the focus of civic life, as opposed to the private spaces, cul-de-sacs, or "dead-ends" that comprise a suburb and where nearby strip malls are the only space to interact (and usually that interaction takes place with a store clerk).

The gymnasium of St. Patrick's Youth Center provided the perfect civic and public space to construct *Higher Ground*. This gym, built in the 1950s, is home to the residents as a place to play basketball after school, do homework, play bingo, and throw parties. The space has an association, for neighborhood residents, as a central place just outside their apartments to play, dance and release energy. For the event, Mary, as designer and chief decorator, began collecting items from the area: Chinese lanterns, votive candles, garlands, and Christmas lights. She created a festive feel within an everyday setting. Our DJ, Steven Harvey, spun records as the audience entered the space, evoking a high-energy dance climate. The audiences at *Higher Ground* were free to dance before and after our show. I had rounded up "icebreakers," or dancing extras—uninhibited souls who got the crowd up and moving; they created the right "climate" out of which the company's dance would erupt. I broke from the traditional dance run—Thursday to Sunday— and performed the project every Saturday night for a month. We only charged five dollars at the door (and continued to do so in subsequent years) to make the event accessible to a wide audience income level. This would be the only place where a family of four could come to a dance "concert" for $20.00! People came back two or three times on different Saturdays. It confirmed my idea that people need and want a way to "get into" concert dance, a way that is less intellectualized, intimidating, and more kinetic. I felt I had made a small dent in rearranging how people receive culture.

We have gone on to tour *Higher Ground* across the U.S.A. in parks, clubs, gymnasiums, community centers, Elk's lodges, and train stations. What proved interesting for the presenters, and is something I had hoped for, was the opportunity for them to "cross the tracks." Presenters had to find a local club (many had never been to their local clubs); they also had to find a DJ (which wasn't so easy either). The combination of a more public space (as opposed to a theater), a DJ (who brings a following of club-goers, many who have never seen modern dance), a local decorating team (who uses decor indigenous to the town), and the dancing extras (the local dancers who serve as icebreakers to get the audience up and moving), provide incredible access to people who said they could never "understand" modern dance or had never actually been inside a theater.

I never set out to do "community" work in the arts. The project evolved from the inside out, meaning it started with my body and the energy that came with my dancing. "Modern dance," the dance we associate with Isadora Duncan, was developed as a humanist form. I question why most of the population began to regard it as elitist and esoteric. I also question the separation, in our culture, of places where we dance, places where we watch dance, places where we eat and drink, and places we associate with spiritual renewal. Bali changed my vision of this. In Bali, the boundaries between these compartments are fluid, the edges are porous. *Higher Ground*, when presented in the church as *The Miracle on Mulberry Street*, attempted to marry seemingly uncommon genres such as social and concert dance, traditional and modern dance. I have been asked if it is necessary to change or simplify the dance for the "general public." Absolutely not. I—we—don't have to "dumb down" work in order to participate in the culture at large. Mary and I have worked to create a transcendent environment within an everyday setting. By removing the proscenium frame, people intuit the dance on a purely physical level. I am free to concentrate on musicality and choreographic complexity without ever having to compromise the dance. In fact, that is the point, the exhilarating thing to experience. The "miracle" for me is witnessing a diverse crowd of "nondance" and "dance-informed" audiences together, moving.

the body

I have developed what I call an ecstatic or precise-abandonment dance style. This way of whipping and cursive dancing never seemed appropriate when there was a "fourth wall." It seemed strange that people would sit in seats far away to witness me, or the other performers dancing and moving, while they themselves remained in the same place. It has always made me feel as if I were pushing out of my skin. "Dancing places," like the historic Roseland, were the places I wanted to dance, not places where people only watched me. On the proscenium stage, the performer is illustrating a state. I prefer to construct an environment where we—all of us, performers *and* audience—"experience" the state. Why can't there be a dancing climate created with the right conditions for all to be moved physically and emotionally? It seems so natural, since we all have the common experience of possessing a body, whether trained or untrained.

My body is only a medium, and my task is to follow and make sense of the precision of its own ability to let go and trust it. This involves negotiating gravity. I was trained in the [Doris] Humphrey dance style, and though I thought I had rebelled against that particular style, the words "fall and recovery" seem to have become the two dominating factors in my dance, and in my life.

This negotiation of gravity between the body's desire to fall and the mind's ability to recover, or vice versa, has endlessly fascinated me. I have never been a choreographer with the ability to write out a dance's spatial patterns, or intellectualize its meaning before the fact. I choose directions and facings by where the body decides to "swing." When working with a company of other dancers, my inclinations lead to dancer-driven choreography. I try to have the choreography reflect, structurally, the ebb and flow of each dancer's body. I have always thought that there were two kinds of choreography, one where the choreography serves the dancers and another where the dancer serves the choreography. My work falls into the first category. I am always aiming to sculpt the swing and sway of the body, including those of others as I watch them work, and learn the ways they move. I have found spaces where that can happen, where audiences can see the body's possibilities close-up, can "feel" the precise abandonment, can use the dancer and the dance as a way to understand their own fall and recovery, chaos and conflicts, as metaphor and as a form of physical activity that is as real as the humans who do it.

paradise

Carrying my ideas of communal dance further, I am drafting interview questions for a large-scale project called *Paradise*. I want to present the piece in a New York City park. My company and I plan to create an interactive arcadia much like the one described in Dan Graham's essay "Garden as Theater as Museum": "The first Italian Renaissance gardens, built astride Roman ruins on hillsides, were sculpture gardens, theaters, archaeological museums, alfresco botanical encyclopedias, educational academies, and amusement parks that drew on special effects to entertain the public.... As 'art forms' they were models of a world intended to be studied."[1] As described in Ovid's poem "Metamorphoses," paradeisos (Greek for "garden" and the root of our present-day "paradise") contained moral, allegorical, scientific, and political lessons. *Paradise* would be such a place, where people can watch dance, dance themselves, and have their eyes and ears filled with image and sound, where people in one geographic location can engage in dialogue with other dance cultures via the World Wide Web.

The project is intended as the culmination of a year's worth of personal research, movement workshops, and conversations. By involving the audience from the beginning, I'll be giving them the tools necessary to express, through word and gesture, their own ideas about utopia. *Paradise*, as I envision it, challenges our limited concept of a traditional dance concert, allowing audience members and performers, over an extended length of time and in a variety of settings, to both inform and be informed, to create and to respond, and ultimately, to begin to approach dance not only on a thematic level, but through shared, kinetic experience.

The initial idea for *Paradise* was to interview people ranging in age from five to ninety-five on their ideas of paradise, personal happiness, and social change. It seems that in any one conversation I have with close friends or acquaintances, people are constantly talking about whether they are doing "okay." As our conversations deepen, individual ideas of social change and visions of a better world begin to emerge. Many of their ideas are not very different from Sir Thomas More's *Utopia*, Edward Bellamy's *Looking Backward*, and H.G.Wells's *A Modern Utopia*; in the worlds these authors created, there are several recurring ideas with socialist undertones. Much of utopian literature was written in reaction to the society in which its authors lived, where they witnessed inequalities and abuse of power. Certain utopias harken back to a way of life freed from the stress of a competitive and commercialized civilization. As an artist reacting to the way art, and more specifically dance, functions in our culture, I look to create a better model. *Paradise* is not about Adam, Eve, and the Garden of Eden; rather it is about my own personal struggle to reposition dance in the cultural framework at large.

THE DANCE

In preliminary workshops, the company will collaborate with a "corps" of twenty-five to one hundred volunteers of varying ages, gathered from my Little Italy neighborhood. Drawing primarily on early American contra dances, in which partners and neighbors swing, pass, and engage one another through a series of "calls," we will meet once a week over the course of a year to create a vocabulary of our own calls. We will then set the movement score for the "audience mixers" that will take place at the event, before and after the concert part of the evening. These workshops will also use ideas based on happenings, improvisation, and club dancing.

The mixers, done to a hip hop/house beat by DJ Steven Harvey, will resemble a large-scale contemporized contra dance led by a designated leader/caller, chosen from the corps. Before and after the concert, the corps will invite members from the audience to learn, participate in, and add to the movement score. Where social dancing evolved into squares, couples, and finally individuals, we want to return to the precursor of those forms, when people danced in large groups. As a remedy to our hyperindividualized state, these contra dances, through their patterns and repetitions, make it possible, in the course of a single dance, for one to meet and engage with fifty to one hundred people.

The concert segment, performed by Sarah Skaggs Dance Company, will erupt out of, and flow back into, the movement score; that part of the evening will continue for forty-five minutes of nonstop movement. Structured in six sections, the piece will express individual ideas of a higher place. The choreography is informed by the previously mentioned ecstatic and cursive vocabulary I've developed over the past twelve years in the studio, and which has been aided and influenced by my travels to the Far East and Eastern Europe.

THE MUSIC

Steven Harvey, who has created sound scores for me for the past twelve years, is also a visual art curator and musicologist; he draws from a wide variety of musical forms traditionally associated with dance and dancing (club, swing, techno, drumming, etc.), weaving common threads between seemingly different genres. This continuum of rhythm will lay the foundation for the corps-and-audience mixers.

THE VISUALS

Within the following large-scale technological arena, ephemeral yet core issues may emerge: the actual construction of our notions of physical and spiritual perfection; the universal implications of individual ideas of peace and happiness; the continuity and overlap of our ideas of paradise over time and space.

Working with videographer Gary Pozner to capture the conversations and movements of the workshop participants, these interviews will provide one of the foundations of the dance, oscillating between the individual and the collective. During the event, an edited version will be projected onto four drive-in movie sized screens (20 feet each) with the help of multimedia designer, Nancy Westcott, with whom I've worked for over a decade.

Mary Gearhart will structure three concentric circles out of light, symbolizing three interconnected realms of passage: the past, the present, and the future. The four 20-foot screens will surround the perimeter of the park as the outer ring. The middle ring will be marked by a string of lights that envelopes the audience space. A cluster of ten halogen lights will define the concert space within the innermost ring.

People will arrive at dusk, to find a party in progress. Mr. Harvey will be spinning records, the video montage will be running, people will be dancing, wandering, and socializing. After the sun has set, and the dancing energy has reached a peak, the first mixer will materialize. As the DJ spins his final tune for the opening segment, it will signal the beginning of the forty-five-minute concert. The corps will then initiate the final mixer, enticing more and more audience members into the dance. The distinction between those who *watch* and those who *do* is narrowed, and the park comes alive with thousands of people dancing, and engaging one another.

From early on in *Cross Cultural Studies* (1984) and *Higher Ground* (1993) to the present, my connecting thread has always been to bring seemingly different vocabularies and voices together, creating dance events that stretch boundaries. I want to involve as many people as participants as I can, and give new meaning to the word *recreation*.

note

1   Dan Graham, "Garden as Theater as Museum." In *Rock My Religion: Writings and Art Projects 1965–1990*. (Cambridge, MA: The MIT Press, 1993), 286–87.

—1996/1997

commentary

IMAGE

A diamond-tipped, platinum arrow is shot skyward, trailed by the woman who shot it. She is sleek as a wet woodland animal. As the arrow goes higher and higher, she yelps with joy and fear in equal measure, holding on with one hand. With the other, she carries a throng of people wrapped in rags and shiny baubles, faces bright with anticipation and wonder. She cannot look down, or she fears they will all fall. She flies up and up, eyes focused determinedly on the heavens until she has redeemed herself, and all of them, from the tyrannical perfection of gravity.

REFLECTION

Sarah Skaggs's "Paradise Remixed" is, in part, utopist text, a map or plan, a path toward one possible reading and redefinition of cultural work. Skaggs's use of spoken text within her performance work is limited, defined by the communal decisions she makes with longtime collaborators, confined to prerecorded popular music or, on occasion, found movie text; where Skaggs has used opera, as in her solo, *Callas,* (1989), her movements made it possible, while not being a literal rendering, to "transmit" the music, created a way in, a permeable membrane. Her work has grown ever more populist in intention since that time, meant to be accessible to the widest possible range of classes, ethnic groups, ages, and numbers of audience as participants. Described textually, its sophistication of approach and result in its usual placement within the medium and milieu of dance does not become immediately apparent.

Skaggs's project is not merely about getting people up and moving. Trained and highly skilled, she wants to ensure that her choreography and dancing may be seen and understood by more than a small coterie of cognoscenti. It is a stance both ethical and practical. It is this *integration* of formal dance concerns *within* a framework of social dance events that is its defining characteristic. When Skaggs's company warms up on the dance floor amid everyone else, and dances among everyone later, it alters conditions of awe or intimidation existing between the passive spectator and the active performer; through closure of the physical space between them, it opens the representational or symbolic. That aspect is an ambitious reformulation of an existing idea about the function of dance as a tool for building cooperation and engendering unity.[1] Skaggs, however, insists upon the potential of all not only to participate, but to understand *as spectators*, at a certain point in the proceedings, the *formal aspects* of postmodern work. The idea is Brechtian in its implications.[2]

Skaggs's project is messianic, her text in *Footnotes* both prescription and description, written with candor in artless, unambiguous prose meant to show—as photographs from a journey might—the manner in which one woman threads her way through the world as both singular person and paradigm. Skaggs does not want to mystify or threaten. She communicates in a straightforward, anyone-can-get-where-I'm-coming-from manner. She is not the dancer-as-writer; she is the dancer-as-dancer, one not interested in replacing the terrain of dance with the territory of words. She is also the dancer as citizen. The issues with which she struggles, as citizen and choreographer/performer are not neatly defined answers to complex questions. As a text, hers is not meant as a substitute for the impulse and passion of live performance; her discourse with the culture is held in the language in which Skaggs is most fluent and expressive, that of the lived and dancing body. This is not to say that in the current context a certain facet of her position is not clear. It is: she has traveled and seen a better way, and she wants to bring it back home and foment a bloodless, but radical, revolution, one that will bring people to their own sense of self through pleasure in *communitas*; she wants to awaken them, have them pay attention to their own aspirations through an inspired dialogue not only with one another, but with a collectively-witnessed art form.

The "Paradise" section of "Paradise Remixed" is a read-between-the-lines examination of a state of desire. It is a proposal as expression of doubt and dare, a request to hundreds of people to come out and rejoice. Although artists often receive the message that such large-scale, inclusive projects will garner support, and propose them for that reason, Skaggs is not this manner of strategist, or cynic. Utopia, for Skaggs, is sensed first, but not exclusively, in the act of dancing; its possibilities are reinforced by day-to-day encounters with people, artists and non-artists alike. All artists have this experience, but most retreat from its implications once back in the studio, and in response to the pressures of career building and the presentation of work. Skaggs, on the other hand, has been affected by these experiences; they have changed her perceptions about the relationship of art to society, the very ways in which she considers where she will place her work. It has been heightened by her experiments with neighborhood dance events, buttressed by her readings of socialist-utopian texts, and revealed as an impossible-to-articulate yearning.

Skaggs is convinced of the efficacy of dance as a way to break through or modify limitations in regard to social structures. She does not examine the darker sides of utopian experiments; that is not her beat. In regard to Skaggs's *Paradise* project, one can think of rock concerts as apt analogy. She understands the power of such events to wrest people from apathy. The band members send out the original thrust of energy; what happens to the crowd is a ripple effect; it is the person standing next to you, and the next and the next and the next, that is responsible for the "electric" transmission that takes place. The same can be said of a riot—a mob scene—but it is this potential for release Skaggs wishes to harness and apply toward nonviolent ends.

Skaggs works in relation to what she knows, to dance, attempting to go beyond the view of the body as merely a finite unit. Seen only as such, the body is a stand-in for the myth of individualism in a culture that prides itself on the efficacy of that particular myth, and has a difficult time accepting information from subcultures with more communal frames of reference. The individual body as symbol of *individualism* delimits the potential for extrapolating the individual from the whole. Skaggs seems to imply that the body's physical enclosure may deceive, make one forget that we are, conceptually, part of something larger. Her analysis of suburbia reflects this point. Its initial intention was that of reward, post-World War II, for a job well done. It is the middle classes regarding physical privacy — usually, the privilege of the aristocracy—as a sought-after ideal. In the 1960s and 1970s, it was a retreat from urban areas undergoing upheaval. Its subtext was that a problem did not require or involve communal solutions, but was the province of those who had no choice but to stay put. It was color-coded.

Skaggs would like to take the trance dances that exist in other cultures and not so much transplant them as use the fact of their existence to consider states of exultation. She is responding to repressive elements within our own culture that view pleasure as sin, countering it by adhering to her utopian project, with its elements of Dionysian bacchanal. She does not purport to present herself as political analyst, but as a cultural worker whose training qualifies her to inform others in specific ways: "Mary [Gearhart] and I have worked to create a transcendent environment within an everyday setting"(p. 153).

Skaggs conflates the political with the spiritual in an ironic mirroring of the conflation of democracy with capitalism. She has always struck me as *echt* American, a holdout— though too young chronologically to be considered one of the children of the Vietnam era— of those who felt themselves to be the true patriots by sensing the unease and sorrow of a populace which, while constantly being told how happy and lucky they were, and objectively fortunate in many respects, were simultaneously distanced, fragmented, and lacking an individual and group sense of self. Her text is *about.* Her project is thing-in-itself. She is involved not in answers, but in posing the question that those in modern and postmodern dance often ask: Who, and where are the people, and how can I dance for them?

AFTERIMAGE

A woman, face subtly mobile, hair flying, lips moving barely perceptibly as if in dialogue with an unseen partner, tears across an empty space, responding to silent messages, revelations.

notes

1   Anna Halprin, West Coast dance experimentalist and mentor to several of those who formed the original core of the Judson Church group has, since the 1950s, created and continues to create work—and rituals—for extensive numbers of people, many or most of whom are nondancers; Deborah Hay began working with large groups of dancers and nondancers in the 1960s.

2   Bertolt Brecht (1898–1956), the German playwright and poet, evolved a theater of political and social criticism. Part of his strategy, briefly stated, was to create an openness, or receptivity, in the spectator so that the underlying political message of his work would not meet with resistance.

selected
bibliography

Adshead-Lansdale, Janet, and June Layson, eds. *Dance History: An Introduction*. London and New York: Routledge, 1983.

Bachmann, Ingeborg. *The Thirtieth Year*. New York: Holmes & Meier, 1987.

Banes, Sally. *Terpsichore in Sneakers: Post-Modern Dance*. Boston: Houghton Mifflin, 1980.

Banes, Sally. *Writing Dancing in the Age of Postmodernism*. Hanover, NH: Wesleyan University Press/University Press of New England, 1994.

Baudrillard, Jean. *America*. Translated by Chris Turner. London and New York: Verso, 1988.

Benjamin, Walter. *Illuminations*. New York: Schocken Books, 1969

Bishop, Elizabeth. *The Complete Poems, 1927–1979*. New York: Farrar, Straus & Giroux, 1995.

Bloch, Ernst. *The Utopian Function of Art and Literature: Selected Essays*. Translated by Jack Zipes and Frank Mecklenburg. Cambridge, MA: The MIT Press, 1988.

Campbell, Joseph. *The Masks of God: Primitive Mythology*. New York: Penguin, 1969.

Creeley, Robert. *The Gold Diggers and Other Stories*. New York: Scribner, 1965.

Darton, Eric. *Free City*. New York: W.W. Norton, 1996.

Derrida, Jacques. *Acts of Literature*. Edited by Derek Attridge. New York and London: Routledge, 1992.

Ellison, Ralph. *Invisible Man*. New York and London: Penguin, 1952.

Erasmus, Charles J. *In Search of the Common Good: Utopian Experiments Past and Future*. New York: Macmillan, 1977.

Foster, Susan Leigh ed. *Corporealities: Dancing Knowledge, Culture and Power*. London and New York: Routledge, 1996.

Foucault, Michel. *The Use of Pleasure: The History of Sexuality*, vol. 2. New York: Random House, 1986.

Fraleigh, Sondra Horton. *Dance and the Lived Body: A Descriptive Aesthetics*. Pittsburgh: University of Pittsburgh Press, 1987.

Goldstein, Joseph. *Insight Meditation: The Practice of Freedom*. Boston and London: Shambhala, 1994.

Gordimer, Nadine. *The Essential Gesture: Writing, Politics, and Places*. Edited by Stephen Clingman. London: Penguin, 1988.

Halprin, Anna. *Moving Toward Life, Five Decades of Transformational Dance*. Hanover and London: University Press of New England, 1995.

Hine, Daryl, and Joseph Parisi eds. *The Poetry Anthology, 1912–1977*, Boston: Houghton Mifflin, 1978.

Homer. *The Iliad*. Translated by Michael Reck. New York: Harper Collins, 1994.

Homer. *The Odyssey*. Translated by Walter Shewring. Oxford and New York: Oxford University Press, 1980.

Kafka, Franz. *The Complete Stories*. Edited by N. Glatzer. New York: Schocken Books, 1971.

Kristeva, Julia. *Desire in Language, A Semiotic Approach to Literature and Art*. Edited by Leon S. Roudiez, translated by Thomas Gora, Alice Jardine, and Leon S. Roudiez. New York: Columbia University Press, 1980.

Macksey, Richard, and Eugenio Donato, eds. *The Structuralist Controversy*. Baltimore and London: The Johns Hopkins University Press, 1977.

McEvilley, Thomas. *Art & Discontent*. Kingston, NY: McPherson & Company, 1991.

McFee, Graham. *Understanding Dance*. London and New York: Routledge, 1992.

O'Hara, Frank. *Lunch Poems*. San Francisco: City Lights Books, 1964.

Plath, Sylvia. *Ariel*. New York: Harper & Row, 1966.

Rainer, Yvonne. *Yvonne Rainer: Work 1961–73*. Halifax: The Press of the Nova Scotia College of Art and Design; New York: New York University Press.

Rushdie, Salman. *Midnight's Children*. New York: Avon Books, 1982.

Sachs, Curt. *World History of the Dance*. New York: Norton, 1963.

Sekida, Katsuki. *Zen Training, Methods and Philosophy*. New York and Tokyo: Weatherhill, 1985.

Sexton, Anne. *Words for Dr. Y.* Edited by Linda Grey Sexton. Boston: Houghton Mifflin, 1978.

Shakespeare, William. *The Tragedy of Hamlet, Prince of Denmark*. New York: Pocket Books, 1992.

Wittgenstein, Ludwig. *Philosophical Grammar*, Berkeley and Los Angeles: University of California Press.

biographies

Elena Alexander is a lapsed performance artist and dancer. Ms. Alexander wrote original text for all pieces performed by her company, Mad Alex. Solo, or with the company, Ms. Alexander performed at, among others, P. S. 122, Franklin Furnace, P.S. 1, Construction Company, El Taller Latinoamericano (now El Taller) and was the first performance artist ever asked to participate in *Rock Against Racism* at Central Park's Bandshell; in 1984, her company toured Sweden, Holland, and England. She stopped performing as a dancer in 1987. In 1990, her writing appeared in *Seeing in the Dark*, an anthology edited by Ian Breakwell and Paul Hammond and published by Serpent's Tail (London). Subsequently, Ms. Alexander's stories and poems have been published in the anthologies *Aloud: Voices from the Nuyorican Poets Café*, edited by Miguel Algarín and Bob Holman (New York: Henry Holt, 1994), *Brought to Book* edited by Ian Breakwell and Paul Hammond (London: Penguin, 1994), and the periodicals *BOMB*, (1991, 1993, 1996), *Cocodrilo, LUNGFULL!* (1995, 1996, 1998), and *the minnesota review (1998)*. Ms. Alexander has collaborated on the hardcover catalogue *Hotel Series* with visual artist Alan Uglow (Amsterdam: Onrust Publications, 1990), and with photographer Denise Adler, on *Parallel Spell: 7 Pictures/7 Poems* (Prestone Printing Company, 1995). She wrote and delivered a text, and was additionally a panelist, for The Ewald Scholar's

Symposium (hosted that year by the dance department at Sweet Briar College, Virginia, 1991), and was a panelist and poetry reader for the NYC Poetry Talks symposium (New York University, 1996). She has read her work at The Poetry Project at St. Mark's Church, as the "Spotlight" at Nuyorican Poets Cafe, at the Ear Inn, and on radio station WBAI. In 1990, Ms. Alexander, in collaboration with British videographer and cinematographer John Christie, cowrote and directed the short film *Paper House* in the Netherlands; it premiered at Nederlandse Film Dagen, Utrecht. In 1993, Ms. Alexander began curating and sponsoring readings under the auspices of the MAD ALEX Arts Foundation; two series—*MAD ALEX Presents* and *Devotional: Writers' Retrospectives*—take place autum through spring. From 1984 through 1996, Ms. Alexander was on the Board of Directors of The Danspace Project at St. Mark's Church, serving as board president from 1987 to 1991.

Jill Johnston's public career as a writer began in 1959 at *The Village Voice*, where she wrote criticism—on dance, mainly, but also on art, happenings, music, and books—until 1965. Simultaneous during this period was her work as a monthly reviewer for *Art News*. From 1965–1975 she had a second career at the *Voice*, writing her own columns, which became increasingly political by 1970; she continued on at the paper until 1980, regularly contributing articles and reviews. The early 1970s saw the publication of three of Johnston's books: *Marmalade Me* (Dutton), *Lesbian Nation* (Simon and Schuster), and *Gullible's Travels* (Links Books). Throughout all of this time she contributed to numerous magazines and quarterlies, and lectured throughout the U.S. on art, politics, and writing. In 1983 and 1985 respectively, *Mother Bound* and *Paper Daughter*, both autobiographies, were published by Alfred A. Knopf.

Since 1985 Johnston has been a regular contributor of articles and reviews to the *New York Times Book Review*. In November 1994, Chicago Review Press published her *Secret Lives in Art: Essays on Art, Literature, Performannce, 1984–94*, and in October 1996 *Jasper Johns: Privileded Information* was published by Thames and Hudson. A revised and expanded edition of *Marmalade Me* was published by Wesleyan University Press/University Presses of New England in 1998, and forthcoming from Serpent's Tail Press in March of 1998 is *Admission Accomplished: The Lesbian Nation Years 1970–75*.

Douglas Dunn danced with Merce Cunningham & Dance Company (1968–1973), Yvonne Rainer & Group (1968–1970), and Grand Union

(1970–1976). He began presenting his own work in 1971, formed Douglas Dunn & Dancers in 1978*, and in 1980 was commissioned by the Autumn Festival and the Paris Opera Ballet to choreograph Igor Stravinsky's *Pulcinella* on the Paris Opera Dancers as part of an homage to the composer. He continues to make new dances for his own and other ballet and modern groups, and to perform with his troupe in the U.S. and abroad. Collaborators over the years include, in film and video: Charles Atlas, and Rudy Burckhardt; in design, Charles Atlas, Mimi Gross, David Ireland, Uli Gassmann, Jeffrey Schiff, David Hannah, Tal Streeter, and Christian Jaccard; in music, Joshua Fried, Bill Cole, Steve Lacy, Jacob Burckhardt, David Ireland, Alvin Lucier, Steve Kramer, Robert Elam, Yaz Shehab, Lindsey Vickery and Jonathan Mustard, John Driscoll, Linda Fisher, Ron Kuivila, Robert Ashley, and Eliane Radigue; in poetry, Anne Waldman, and Reed Bye; in lighting design: Carol Mullins, Jeffrey McRoberts, Patrick O'Rourke, and Kevin Dreyer.

*Douglas Dunn & Dancers, Rio Grande Union, Inc., 541 Broadway, New York, NY 10012
    Tel:(212)-966-6699; Fax: (212)-274-1804.

Marjorie Gamso grew up in New York City where as a child in the early 1950s she staged live versions of the TV show *Your Hit Parade* with friends in the living rooms of their family apartments. As an adolescent in the late fifties, she wandered through side streets in forbidden neighborhoods and immersed herself in sorrowful poems and ponderous philosophical texts that she barely understood as an act of rebellion against the popular culture of the time. Later, as a college student in the sixties, she took up the study of "culture," obtaining a degree in anthropology. She had danced—joining dance clubs, taking dance classes, attending dance concerts—thinking of the activity as no more than a hobby, a personal avocation, until the year 1970, when an opportunity to choreograph presented itself. She made *Octopus City*, a piece with chance elements for eight dancers on a plexiglass platform above a grid of changing colored lights, and dance/intermedia work decisively became her vocation. She has since composed over thirty dance/performance pieces, has taught dance, written texts for dances and about dancing, and has received several grants. Currently she has an ongoing project, *The Enlightenment*, a series of solos for women of various (chronological) ages, each dancing with a lamp that evokes a particular (historical) age. She is also writing a play based on the relationshp between Hannah Arendt and Martin Heidegger.

Ishmael Houston-Jones's improvised dance and text work has been performed in New York City, across the United States, and in Canada, Europe, and Latin America. He has collaborated with writer Dennis Cooper; filmmaker Julie Dash; visual artists Huck Snyder, Robert Flynt, John DeFazio, Nayland Blake, and with Fred Holland, with whom he shared a New York Dance and Performance "Bessie" Award. Houston-Jones's essays, performance texts, and fiction have appeared in: *Out of Character, Caught in the Act, Performance Talk, Best American Gay Fiction: Volume Two, Contact Quarterly, FARM, Porn Free, Mirage,* and *Movement Research Journal.*

Kenneth King is a dancer/choreographer and writer, who, as Artistic Director of Kenneth King & Dancers/Company, has presented a wide variety of multimedia dance theater, text and performance works at such venues as Judson Church and Gallery, the Brooklyn Academy of Music, the Museum of Modern Art, P.S. 122, Walker Art Center, the American Dance Festival, The Kitchen, Dance Theater Workshop, The Danspace Project and the Poetry Project (both housed in St. Mark's Church), and at various international venues. His work is discussed at length in Sally Banes's *Terpsichore in Sneakers;* he is a featured choreographer in Connie Kreemer's anthology, *Further Steps, Fifteen Choreographers on Modern Dance* (New York: Harper and Row, 1987), in Michael Blackwood's film *Making Dances,* in Robyn Brentano and Andrew Horn's film, *Space City,* and has appeared in the films of Andy Warhol, Jonas Mekas, and Gregory Markopoulos. He has taught widely in many colleges and universities and his writings have appeared in such publications as *The Young American Writers, The Paris Review, The Chicage Review, Text-Sound Texts, Art & Cinema, Semiotext(e), Shantih: The Literature of Soho, Movement Research Journal, Performing Arts Journal, The New American Arts, The New American Cinema, Dance Magazine, Ballet Review,* and in the anthology *Merce Cunningham: Dancing in Space and Time.* He has received fellowships from The John Simon Guggenheim Memorial Foundation, the National Endowment for the Arts, the New York Foundation for the Arts, and the Creative Public Service Program; his company has received grants from the National Endowment for the Arts, the New York State Council on the Arts, the Gallery Association of New York, and the Foundation for Contemporary Performance Arts.

Yvonne Meier comes from Zurich, Switzerland. Since 1979, she has lived and worked in New York City, where she has shown her work at such places as The

Kitchen, Movement Research at Judson Church, P.S. 122, and P.S. 1, as well as in many places outside of the New York area, and in Europe. She has worked with DANCENOISE (Annie Iobst and Lucy Sexton), and often collaborates with Ishmael Houston-Jones and with Jennifer Monson. She has received a number of fellowships, including those from the National Endowment for the Arts, the New York Foundation for the Arts, and NEA Inter-Arts Grants for works such as *Pommes Fritz*, *The Body Snatcher*, and *The Shining*. In 1993, she received a "Bessie" (New York Dance and Performance Award), in choreography, for *The Shining*. Since 1982, she has been a teacher of the Skinner Releasing Technique.

Sarah Skaggs has been choreographing her own work since 1983. Her early dance training includes composition, technique and improvisation with Eija Celli at Sweet Briar College in Virginia, where she was awarded a B.A. with honors in Combined Dance and Drama. She performed in New York and toured around the world with Dana Reitz and Dancers from 1981 to 1985, and collaborated with Reitz and sculptor James Turrell in *Severe Clear*. Ms. Skaggs' work has been produced in New York City by Lincoln Center's Serious Fun! Festival, The Joyce Theater, P.S. 122, The Kitchen, The Danspace Project at St. Mark's Church, and Roulette, as well as many national and international venues. She has received six Choreography Fellowships from the National Endowment for the Arts and two from the New York Foundation for the Arts. From 1989 to 1992, she traveled with the P.S. 122 Field Trips and also traveled and taught in Hong Kong, Taiwan, Holland and Prague as part of the 1993 Dance Theater Workshop Suitcase Fund. She traveled to Bali in 1992, where she studied Legong Dance. In the spring of 1994, her company, Sarah Skaggs Dance, was invited to Prague and Hong Kong to collaborate and create movement exchanges with dancers from those respective countries. These efforts resulted in *Folked Up* which premiered at the Joyce Theater in 1995. In 1996, Ms. Skaggs presented her yearly event, *Miracle on Mulberry Street*, and performed selections from her planned evening-length solo project at The Danspace Project at St. Mark's Church as part of the APAP Festival. She has been working on *Paradise*, a large-scale, interactive dance and film event.